John S. Jenness

Notes on the First Planting of New Hampshire

And on the Piscataqua Patents

John S. Jenness

Notes on the First Planting of New Hampshire
And on the Piscataqua Patents

ISBN/EAN: 9783337268183

Printed in Europe, USA, Canada, Australia, Japan

Cover: Foto ©ninafisch / pixelio.de

More available books at **www.hansebooks.com**

NOTES

ON THE

FIRST PLANTING

OF

NEW HAMPSHIRE

AND ON THE

PISCATAQUA PATENTS.

JOHN S. JENNESS.

PRIVATELY PRINTED.

PORTSMOUTH:
PRINTED BY LEWIS W. BREWSTER.
1878.

THE FIRST PLANTING OF NEW HAMPSHIRE.

WHETHER the first settlement within the limits of New Hampshire was made at Little Harbor near the mouth of the Piscataqua, or at Dover Neck some six miles up the river, is a question which has long employed the studies and pens of our local antiquaries, and of late has found its way into the discussions and acts of our Legislature. Each of these localities has its warm partizans, who have brought to the controversy research and ingenuity in such equal measure, that the question seems, indeed, to have been buried still deeper in doubt and obscurity by their confusing speculations. It is much to be regretted that uncertainty should rest over the most interesting of all periods in the history of our state, that of its birth and infancy; and we feel that an effort to clear away this uncertainty and to bring out into the light the truthful picture of those earliest days, will well be worth the making.

The date of the settlement upon the promontory, now called Odiorne's Point, at the smaller mouth of the Piscataqua river, is not a matter of dispute. Mr. David Thomson, a resident of Plymouth, England, having procured from the Grand Council of Plymouth, Nov. 15, 1622, a patent for six thousand acres of land to be selected by him in New England, sailed from Plymouth in mid-winter with a handful of colonists in the good ship called the "Jonathan of Plymouth," (the Mayflower of New Hampshire,) and arrived at the Piscataqua in the early spring of 1623. Mr. Thomson's design was to found a plantation, convenient for trade and the fisheries, somewhere near the mouth of the Piscataqua river, and as he had visited New England in previous years, and was familiar with the coast, it seems probable that the site of his settlement had been determined upon before he left England upon his present enterprise. David Thomson is described by Morton in *The New England Canaan*," published in 1637 as being "a scottish gentleman, that was conversant with those people (the natives) a scholar and traveller that was diligent in taking notice of these things, as a man of good judgment."

The original agreement or indenture, under which Thomson came over, was recovered several years ago among the ancient Winthrop papers, and has recently been published by Charles Deane, Esq., accompanied by copious and learned notes.

From this it appears that Thomson had three Plymouth merchants as partners or co-adventurers with him in his enterprise, named Abraham Colmer, Nicholas Sherwill and Leonard Pomerie, who were to contribute to the expenses of founding and carrying on the new plantation, and to share in its property at the expiration of the partnership. David Thomson's colony, which first landed with him at Little Harbor, comprised probably not more than ten men.

The indenture referred to provides that the little colony "so landed, shall and will use their best endeavor (by the direccon of said David Thomson) with as much conveniencie as maye be, to find out ****** some fitt place to settle and Builde some houses or buildings for habitacons, on which they are to begin with as muche expedicon as they maye; to the lymits and precincts of which habitacons or buildings soe intented to be there erected, there shall be allotted of the lands next thereunto adjoininge, at or before the end of five years next ensuing the date hereof, the full quantitie of six hundred acres of land or neere thereabouts."

In pursuance of this clause of the Indenture, Thomson and his men selected the Point at Little Harbor as a "fitt place to build their houses for habitacons" and began upon them with as much *expedicon* as they could. The site selected for the settlement was chosen with excellent judgment.

From the Little Harbor fronting the north side of the promontory a salt water creek runs back so far towards the ocean, as almost to convert the enclosed point into an island of about six hundred acres area, which was the precise amount of land required by the Indenture to be allotted to the new plantation. The soil is good, and among the rocks on the harbor shore is a living spring of fresh water. The harbor is safe and accessible at all times to vessels of light draught, and most commodiously situated for the prosecution of the fisheries, as well as for the peltry traffic with the Indians of Sagamore Creek and Piscataqua river. Above all other advantages in those perilous times, the Point, rising on every side towards its centre and almost surrounded by water, was easily defensible against the assaults of savages. These considerations probably determined Thomson in the selection of this site for the new plantation, which he named, perhaps from the Indian appellation, "Pannaway"— a name, which seems however not to have survived the period of Thomson's own occupation and ownership of the plantation.

The principal dwelling house erected at Pannaway was built of stone, and of considerable size. Hubbard informs us that "the chimney and some part of the stone wall were standing in his day" (1680). The house, which, a few years after its erection, passed into the hands of Capt. John Mason and his associates, was afterwards called by these proprietors "Piscataqua House," and sometimes in popular parlance, "Captain Mason's stone house." It was never designated, we believe, Mason's Hall, though Hubbard and his followers have stated to the contrary. The term "Mason's Hall" was sometimes though rarely applied to the "Great House" at Strawberry Bank, erected by the adventurers of Laconia about 1631.*

Thomson's House, erected in 1623 at Pannaway, seems from its remains to have been laid upon a foundation of sea sand and small stones packed close into a trench. The sea sand is identical in appearance with that still abundantly found on the harbor shore in front of the house. There was no cellar beneath the building. The walls above the foundations were built of a slate-like shale laid in blue clay, both of which material are abundant in that immediate neighborhood. Gov. Winthrop built for himself a dwelling house at Mistick of similar material a few years later.† When not greatly exposed to the rain, the tough clay of Little Harbor is as durable as the best mortar. The chimney of the ancient Jaffrey house at New Castle, as Mr. Albee, its present occupant, informs us, was laid in this clay two centuries ago, and still stands strong and solid.

---
*See Jenness Orig. Docs. relating to New Hampshire.
†1 Winthrop 63.

With these materials close at hand, Thomson and his colony could have erected a comfortable and spacious habitation in a short time after their landing. Little or nothing would have been required from England for that purpose beyond window glass, hardware and household utensils. The site of the Pannaway house is still confidently pointed out by the present owners of the territory, and part of the foundation walls are believed to have been exposed by the excavations for a road, which, about thirty years ago, was laid out from the main highway to the harbor. Close by the house, the foundations of a small building, supposed to have been a blacksmith's shop, are pointed out. Among its debris have been recently found, by very slight excavations along the road-side, charcoal and ashes, nails, pieces of iron, a pipe-stem, etc, and also, strange to relate, parts of a human skeleton. No doubt, several other buildings were erected around the principal dwelling, such as a cooper's shop, a carpenter's shop, storehouses, boat houses and barns, but no remains of these have as yet been discovered.

The fishing stages and fish houses, we conjecture, were put up in the sheltered coves upon the ocean side of the point, and in close proximity to *Flake Hill* as it is called, where, according to tradition, the fish were dried. In one of these coves are still to be seen numbers of wooden spiles driven into the sand, which once served, probably, as a foundation for fish houses or boat houses. Between Flake Hill and the main building lies a well filled cemetery, which holds all that remains of the first settlers of New Hampshire. From the long space between the head stones and foot stones, many of which are still standing, this cemetery seems to have been a grave yard of men. We found no small graves in this ancient *God's Acre*. Nature herself has erected a most appropriate monument to the memory of the hardy, daring men who laid the foundations of our state amid the dangers and privations of the wilderness, and have here at last taken up their rest. Out of the very graves near the centre of the small cemetery rises a rugged gnarled walnut tree, bent and distorted in its struggles of two centuries against the elements—a memorial and symbol of the courage and fortitude of the ancient Pannaway men, whose long slumbers the noble tree defiantly protects.

Pannaway house must have been a structure of considerable size to have afforded accommodation to Thomson and his new colony; and as it was put up by ordinary English workmen, we may reasonably conjecture, that it followed the general plan and presented the general appearance of the dwelling houses of the time of James I., vast numbers of which still remain in good preservation all over the old country. As soon as his buildings were put in habitable condition, Thomson entered actively into the prosecution of his enterprise at the Piscataqua, and he continued engaged in that business at Pannaway until about the expiration of the stipulated term of co-partnership with the Plymouth Merchants, in Nov. 1627.

Pannaway plantation became at once well known along the New England coast, and was visited within its very first year by many of the most interesting and striking characters connected with our early history. Phinehas Pratt came there as early as May, 1623, and before the great crackling fires of a cold spring, recounted, no doubt, the story of the terrible winter he had passed at Wessaguscus; of his marvellous escape from the murderous savages across a trackless frozen forest for near fifty miles into New Plymouth in quest of succor, and of the valiant achievements of the redoubtable Miles Standish, who, with a small band of soldiers, set out the very next day from the Pilgrim village, and slaying Pecksuot, the savage chief, with his own hand, succeeded in dispersing the Indians and rescuing the trembling, exhausted planters of Wessaguscus from impending annihilation.

A month or two later, came into Pannaway a half-drowned, half-naked man, imploring succor and protection. He proved to be Mr. Thomas Weston, the faithful friend and agent of the Pilgrim fathers in England before they sailed away for the new world, though at present they entertained towards him sentiments of distrust and unkindliness. His political and religious sentiments did not accord with those of the separatists at New Plymouth. Weston had now been cast away, while cruising along the New Hampshire coast between Boar's Head and Merrimack river; his shallop was wrecked, and himself afterwards assailed and stripped of his clothes by the Indians. The miserable man succeeded at last, however, in making his way along the coast into Pannaway, and there he was clad and restored to health and furnished with means to return to Plymouth.

About this same time, the Pilgrim hero, Miles Standish himself, made his appearance at Pannaway. "Standish," says Hubbard, "had been bred a soldier in the Low countries and never entered the school of Christ or of John the Baptist, or if ever he was there, he had forgot his first lessons. A little chimney is soon fired, so was the Plymouth captain, a man of very small stature yet of a very hot and angry temper."* The valiant captain, at the conclusion of his stout achievements in the rescue of Wessaguscus, was employed to buy provisions at the eastward "for the refreshing of the Plymouth colony." He must have been at Pannaway about the last of June, as he returned to Plymouth in July, laden with the provisions he

---
*Hubbard N. E. p. 84.

was in quest of, and bringing along in his company our Mr. David Thomson from Pannaway.*

The next important visitor at Pannaway was Capt. Christopher Levett, "his majesty's woodward for Somersetshire," as he describes himself. Levett's design was to establish a city at some eligible spot along the New England coast, to be named "York," after the metropolitan city in England, and to found there, in all pomp and circumstance, a full prelatical establishment over all New England. Capt. Levett was an officer in the royal navy, high in favor at court, and of much distinction in the old country. He stayed at Pannaway about a month during the early spring of 1624, awaiting the arrival of his men, to begin his search along the coast for some suitable site for his projected city.

While Levett still remained at Pannaway, Governor Robert Gorges arrived there with a considerable company. Robert Gorges was the son of Sir Ferdinando Gorges and "like his father, of an active enterprising genius, and had newly returned from the Venetian war."† He came out with a commission under the Great Seal, appointing him "Lieutenant General and Governor of New England," and designating Capt. Christopher Levett, before mentioned, as one of his Council. It was

*Mourt's Relation.
†Belknap, Life of Gorges.

at Pannaway that the ceremony of installing Levett into his high office was performed by Governor Gorges, assisted by three others of his Council, and in the presence of all the people, no doubt, then at the plantation. We may be sure that this ceremony, to which it was desirable to give as much distinction and publicity as possible, was performed in a most imposing manner on that great and stirring day in the annals of Pannaway.

That the Indians were visitors at Pannaway during the very first year of its foundation, appears from the narrative of Phinehas Pratt, who writes that "at the time of his (Capt. Levett) being at Pascataway a sachem or Sagamor gave two of his men, one to Capt. Levett and another to Mr. Thomson:" but one that was there said, "How can you trust those savages? Call the name of one 'Watt Tyler' and the other 'Jack Straw,' after the names of the two greatest Rebills yt ever were in England."

Neither was the society of women wholly lacking at Pannaway during this period. David Thomson's wife resided with him at his new plantation, and it is reasonable to believe that she came not without female companions. And it was here at Pannaway, that John, the son of David, it is believed, first saw the light—the first-born of New Hampshire.

We have thus sketched, as briefly as possible, some of the principal events in the history of Pannaway for the first year of its existence, from the spring of 1623 to the spring of 1624. It is not within the design of this paper to follow its history any further. It will suffice our present purpose to add, that the plantation founded by David Thomson and his co-adventurers at Little Harbor passed in 1630, by way of lease, into the hands of the company of Laconia. It was then that the doughty soldier of fortune, Capt. Walter Neale, the Governor for that company, and the worthy compeer of Miles Standish himself, took possession of Pannaway as his "chiefe habitacon," and thus preserved the nucleus of the future State of New Hampshire.

The Pannaway plantation, the story of whose birth and infancy we have thus outlined, was, we are convinced, prior in date to any other settlement within the limits of our State, and several years anterior to that of Edward Hilton at Dover Point. The earliest period to which the latter settlement can be referred upon any of the testimony which has come down to us, is the year 1628, or possibly the year 1627. If there had been any settlement at Dover Neck prior to that period, there exists the testimony of no contemporary, to the effect that he had visited it or had seen it, or had heard of it from rumor or report. And certainly it is highly improbable that such a settlement could have existed for four or five years up the Piscataqua river, without having been known to the Pilgrim historians, such as Bradford and Winslow, nor once spoken of or referred to by any of the numerous visitors at Pannaway.

If Hilton's Point had been settled as early as 1623, would not the planters and servants employed there have found occasions to meet constantly and familiarly with their countrymen at the thriving plantation of Pannaway only six miles distant? would not the existence of a Hilton's Point colony have been as well and widely known as that of Pannaway itself? And yet no settlement at Hilton's Point until several years subsequent to that of Thomson at Little Harbor, is referred to by any New England writer of that time or in any contemporaneous paper, letter, affidavit or document of any kind. On the contrary, Christopher Levett, Esq. who, as we have seen, spent a month at Pannaway in the early spring of 1624, so far from having heard of any English settlement up the river, writes thus on his leaving for the Eastward: "About two miles further to the East, I found a great river and a good harbor, called Pascattaway, but for the ground I can say nothing, but by the relation of the Sagamore or King of that place, who told me there was much good ground up in the river about seven or eight leagues."*

Certainly, if Hilton had settled a plantation at Dover Neck in 1623, Levett must during his long

---

*2 Maine Hist. Col. p. 80.

visit to David Thomson have heard of such a settlement, and would not have been compelled to rely upon an Indian Sagamore for a description of the Piscataqua river; nor is it likely that he would have passed over without notice so important a circumstance as the foundation there of a new English colony. It is fair to conclude, in the absence of direct testimony on the subject, that up to the time of Levett's visit to Pannaway in 1624, the Piscataqua above its mouth still remained a solitude unbroken by white settlers.

The patent of Hilton's Point was granted to Edward Hilton, March 12, 1629 (1630, according to our present style of reckoning,) about *seven years* after the settlement of Thomson at Pannaway. Can it be believed that Hilton founded a plantation at Hilton's Point, in 1623, *seven years* before he got a deed of the land his plantation stood upon? No great expense would certainly have been incurred by him until he had first acquired title to the soil. Nor did Edward Hilton himself ever to our knowledge make any pretence to having begun a plantation on the Piscataqua at so early a date. The patent granted to him in 1630 recites, as usual with such instruments, the utmost that he claimed to have done at Hilton's Point before that year. The language is this, "that Edward Hilton and his associates hath already at his and their own proper costs and charges transported sundry servants to plant in New England aforesaid at a place there called by the natives Weeanacohunt, otherwise Hilton's Point, lying some two leagues from the mouth of the river Pascataquack in New England aforesaid, where they have already built some houses and planted corn, and for that he does further intend by God's Divine Assistance to transport thither more people and cattle, &c."*

It will be seen that Hilton made no claim to having settled a plantation at Hilton's Point so early as 1623, as he naturally would have done had such been the fact. Nor is their any pretence in the patent that he had *set up fishing stages there*, as Belknap and others, following Hubbard, have asserted. The language of the Grant imports simply that the plantation at Hilton's Point was to be carried on for trade and agriculture, and that feeble beginnings in that direction had been very lately made, to be followed by a more strenuous exertion and a larger outlay upon the acquisition of title to the plantation. Edward Hilton lived on the Piscataqua for many years after founding his plantation, and was a gentleman of energy and probity. His territory was sold by him shortly after he obtained his patent, to Capt. Thomas Wiggin and his associates of Shrewsbury, England.

---

* See Hilton's Point Patent at large, Appendix No. 1.

This patent became for many after years the source of much conflict and litigation. Yet never did Hilton, nor those claiming title under him, undertake to strengthen that title by averring a seven years' possession and actual occupation before his patent was issued.

Positive testimony as to the date of the Hilton's Point settlement may, however, be found in a careful declaration made in 1654 to the Mass. General Court, by John Allen, Nicholas Shapleigh and Thomas Lake, wherein the Hilton's Point Patent is relied upon by the declarants as a protection against certain alleged encroachments made by the Mass. authorities. These three declarants, familiar with the whole history of Hilton's Point and interested to make out Hilton's title and possession as ancient as they could, present the following as the first article of their case. "1, that Mr. Edward Hilton was possessed of this land about the year 1628, which is about 26 years ago." * Edward Hilton was then living in the immediate vicinity of Great Bay, well and intimately known to all the declarants; and the date of his first possession of Hilton's Point must have been within the familiar knowledge of them all.

The notion among our historians and antiquaries that the Dover settlement was contemporaneous with that of Pannaway in the spring of 1623, is

* 1 N. H. Prov. Pap. 157.

founded wholly and solely, so far as we can discover, upon a certain careless statement contained in Hubbard's Hist. of New England, written more than half a century after the settlement of New Hampshire—a loose statement, made upon hearsay, in a paragraph (as printed) conspicuous in all respects for inaccuracy. And worse than all, the little of truth the paragraph of Rev. William Hubbard of Ipswich did contain, has been most grossly distorted and misunderstood. Hubbard's language is this : "Some merchants and other gentlemen in the west of England * * * sent over that year (1623) one Mr. David Thomson with Mr. Edward Hilton and his brother Mr. William Hilton, who had been fishmongers in London, with some others that came along with them, furnished with necessaries for carrying on a plantation there (about Piscataqua River.) Possibly others might be sent after them in the years following 1624 and 1625; some of whom first, in probability, seized on a place called the Little Harbor on the west side of the Piscataqua river, toward or at the mouth thereof; the Hiltons, in the meanwhile, setting up their stages higher up the river toward the northwest at or about a place since called Dover. But at that place called Little Harbor it is supposed was the first house set up that was built in those parts."*

An examination of this statement by Hubbard

---

*Hubbard's Hist. pp. 214, 215.

will satisfy the student that it amounts to this: First, that the *first* house or settlement on the Piscataqua was made at Little Harbor. Second, that the Hiltons set up their stages up the river sometime *in the meanwhile* between 1623 and the years following 1624 and 1625; and Hubbard has not said nor meant to say that Hilton's settlement was made in 1623. Third, that the Hiltons set up their stages at or about a place since called Dover. Hubbard has not stated nor meant to state that these stages were set up *at* Hilton's Point precisely, but only at some place *about* that Point.

A little consideration will convince us that Hubbard could hardly have intended to say that the Hiltons did ever set up *stages at Hilton's Point;* and certainly Hilton himself in the preamble to his grant of 1630 never made any pretence, as we have seen, to having set up any fishing stages there. *The stages* referred to, were large and expensive structures, intended for use in the *fishing business.* Hilton's Point is situated some six or seven miles above the mouth of Piscataqua river —a tidal stream of such rapidity that it is often impossible for a boat to overcome its current, while on the other hand the great codfisheries lie several miles out to sea beyond the river's mouth. A fisherman leaving Hilton's Point at the very turn of the ebb tide, might, perhaps, under favorable circumstances, reach the fishing banks in the course of four hours; if he intended to return by the next flood tide, he would be compelled to turn back without casting a hook. If he stayed two or three hours to fish, he would not be able to get home the same day. Can it be believed that experienced fishermen would have selected such a site as Hilton's Point for a fishing establishment, when as good land or better could have been taken up anywhere at the river's mouth or along the coast?

Where, indeed, it really was that these fishing stages were set up, (if at all,) Hubbard has not definitely informed us, nor can we now discover; but it hardly seems probable that a site was selected above the river *narrows*. Taking the whole case together, we may perhaps conclude from Hubbard's statements, if we chose to place any reliance whatever upon them, *as they stand printed*, that the Hiltons sometime between 1623 and 1626 founded a fishing establishment somewhere up the river between Dover and the river's mouth. This may be the truth, without conflicting in the least with the testimony we have adduced, that the trading and agricultural establishment on Hilton's Point itself was founded by Edward Hilton in the year 1627 or 1628.

We perceive, therefore, that Hubbard is no authority whatever in support of the alleged settlement of Hilton's Point in 1623, and as no other evidence has been adduced to prove such a settlement contemporaneously with that at Pannaway, we may justly consider the question at rest, and accord the priority in the first planting of New Hampshire by several years to David Thomson and his men at Pannaway. Indeed a close scrutiny of Hubbard's statement by the light of other facts will convert his misunderstood narrative into an authority for our conclusion. He tells us that the settlement "at or about a place since called Dover" was made by the *two* Hiltons, Edward and William. If that were so, it could not have been made in the year *1623*, because William is found residing at Plymouth with his family as late as *1624*, and indeed is not mentioned as living on the Piscataqua until several years later.

We venture to add, though unnecessary to our argument, that the time and manner of *Edward* Hilton's arrival in the Piscataqua is also very uncertain. Hubbard writes that both Edward and William came over in company with Thomson in 1623. That the careless historian made a gross error as to *William* we have just pointed out, and it is probable he fell into a similar mistake as to *Edward*. At all events, the Indenture between Thomson and his partners gives no countenance to Hubbard's loose expressions; and not a particle of contemporaneous testimony has been added tending to show Edward Hilton's residence at the Piscataqua before the year 1628, when he first appears as assessed £1 towards the expense of Morton's banishment.

A strong concurrent body of testimony would, indeed, be necessary to satisfy a rational mind, that Edward and William Hilton, or Edward alone settled at Dover Neck as early as 1623. At that period not a white man dwelt within all the borders of New Hampshire, tribes of bloodthirsty "nefandous" savages roamed through the pine forests and gathered around the falls of the rivers. Hilton's Point, from its close proximity to the Cocheco, where large bands of Indians made their homes, was particularly exposed to savage assault. Is it credible that Hilton, without any colony to assist him, (for, as we have seen, no colony came over to Dover Neck until 1628 or 1629,) should have, as early as 1623, removed from the succor of all his friends, six or seven miles from Pannaway, and taken up an almost, if not altogether, solitary residence in the midst of treacherous and cruel savages; when the whole country practically lay open to him to go in and occupy where he would? A wise and prosperous merchant, as Edward Hilton was, a prudent and judicious gentlemen, as he ever afterwards proved himself to be, would never, we believe, have undertaken an enterprise as unnecessary and profitless, as it would have been rash and foolhardy.

It was some years, we conclude, after the settlement of Pannaway, whether we consider the testimony or weigh the intrinsic probabilities, before the plantation at Hilton's Point could have been begun; and it is much to be regretted, that the antiquaries and historians of our State should have permitted the Legislature to fall into the error of incorporating a body of men to erect a monument at Dover Neck, "in commemoration of the settlement of the Point in 1623."

THE PISCATAQUA PATENTS.

In the preceding monograph we have sought to dispel the obscurity which has so long enveloped the very cradle of New Hampshire history. We have endeavored to establish that the first English settlement within the limits of that State was made by David Thomson and his company in 1623, at Pannaway, Little Harbor, about five years earlier than Edward Hilton began his plantation at Hilton's Point, now called Dover Neck

Advancing from this starting point only a few steps further into the early history of New Hampshire, the student is again shut in by a dense fog, through which for a long time he is compelled to grope his uncertain way. Before the year 1632 is passed, he finds himself in the midst of a number of patents on the Piscataqua, none of which can he clearly make out and define. He perceives long and bitter contests between these rival patents, the true ground of which he cannot understand. He discovers that at last all these contending patentees and planters are in some way swept into the jurisdiction of Massachusetts Bay, but the dexterous legerdemain by which the annexation was effected, entirely escapes his detection. In vain does he seek for light in the pages of the Pilgrim or the Puritan historians. That whole confraternity, indeed, avowedly look upon the Piscataqua plantations with utter contempt, and waste little or no time upon the annals of those "sons of Belial," who haunted about the lower part of the river.

Moreover, it happens, as we shall see in the sequel, that it became the policy of the Bay Colony, in prosecuting their designs over the Piscataqua, to say or write as little as possible on the subject, so that in case they should ever be called to account for their conduct in the matter, they could not, in any event, be condemned out of their own mouths.

The true story of the Piscataqua Patents has thus never been told; and, indeed, until the recent discovery of important documents in the English Archives, bearing on the subject, that portion of our early history was incapable of any clear relation.

Let us attempt to dissipate some of the mists which have so long hung over Piscataqua River. Let us enquire what these patents really were, what was their real meaning, what must be their true construction, what conflicting interests arose under them; let us sketch the outlines of their history down to their extinction, and discover, if possible, in what way these patents were at last merged into the Bay Colony. Such an enquiry, in the present state of our knowledge, must needs be delicate and difficult; nor, in so novel an undertaking is it likely to attain absolute success. Our hopes will be fully gratified, if these few pages shall succeed in letting in some measure of light upon this obscure and confused portion of our early history.

The instrument which has been the chief cause of the confusion and obscurity referred to, was the Patent, mentioned in the preceding monograph, granted in 1629-30 by the Grand Council for New England to Edward Hilton and his associates—a petty conveyance of a small tract of land around Dover Neck, but which in the course of events having been elevated into some political importance, played a leading part, as we shall see, in the early annals of New Hampshire.

It was during the years 1628 and 1629, that Mr. Edward Hilton, a member of the ancient and honorable Guild of Fishmongers of London, with the aid of a number of Bristol merchants, put up a few cabins at the Point which took his name, and laid the feeble foundations of a trading and lumbering plantation. This occupation was, it seems, unwarranted by any previous grant of title from the Grand Council; though probably some agreement or understanding had been arrived at, for the execution of a good and sufficient deed of conveyance, as soon as the plantation should be fairly under way. It was not uncommon for the Grand Council to require from petitioners for land in New England, some evidence of efforts already made and expenditures actually incurred towards the improvement of the desired territory, before the patent was actually executed and delivered. As the quitrents on these conveyances were merely nominal, the Council could hardly have hit upon a better way of testing the sincerity and ability of those who solicited from them gratuitous grants for the alleged design of founding plantations in the New World.

Edward Hilton and his associates having in 1628 and 1629 "transported sundry servants to plant upon Hilton's point, now Dover Neck, built some houses, planted corn, etc.," and having thus satisfactorily shown their intention and ability to carry forward the plantation already begun, at length received from the Grand Council a conveyance or Patent for the territory they had taken up. This Patent was executed *March 12, 1629* (old style), or according to our present supputation of time, *March 23, 1630*.*

The territory conveyed to Hilton and his associates by this Patent is bounded and described in the

---
* See the Patent in the Appendix No. 1.

instrument, as follows: "*All that part of the river Pascataquack, called or known by the name of Wecanacohunt or Hilton's Point with the south side of the said river, up to the fall of the river and three miles into the maine land by all the breadth aforesaid.*"

We invite particular study into the true intent and meaning of this brief description, because of the falsification of its terms and the strange distortion of its meaning, which we believe was subsequently put upon the patent by the authorities of Massachusetts Bay; whereby the patent was split into two distinct parts, and a large tract of territory on the southerly or Rockingham County side of the river was, by construction, brought within its limits. To the consideration of this subject in greater detail, we shall return in the sequel, after several other necessary preliminaries have been brought to the student's knowledge.

It seems clear to us, that the terms of the Patent are intended to bound and limit, not *two* entirely separate and disjoined bodies of land, (as Massachusetts afterward contended,) but only the one contiguous compact territory, on which Hilton and his associates *had already begun* their plantation. Such, indeed, is the express declaration of the preamble to the grant. Beginning at Hilton's Point, (now called Dover Neck—a well-defined projection into Piscataqua river,) the boundary line, as we construe the Patent, ran up along the southerly side of that river to the lower or Quampegan Falls—a distance of some seven or eight miles—and reached back into the interior country three miles along the entire river frontage; thus embracing a considerable portion of the present towns of Dover, Rollinsford and Durham, and including the falls of the Cocheco and Oyster rivers.*

Soon after obtaining his Patent, Mr. Edward Hilton returned to the Piscataqua with reinforcements and supplies, and settled down at the Point, which already bore his name. Formal possession or *livery of seizin* was given to him July 7, 1631, by Thomas Lewis.

Hilton's Point, now called Dover Neck, upon which Hilton and his men pitched their settlement, is, in the language of Dr. Belknap, "a high neck of land between the main branch of Pascataqua and Back River, about two miles long and half a mile wide, rising along a fine road and declining on each side like a ship's deck. It commands an extensive and variegated prospect of the rivers, bays, adjacent shores and distant mountains. It has often been admired by travellers as an elegant situation for a city, and by military gentlemen for a fortress."†

---

* See the Sketch Map, *infra*, whereon the territory within these bounds is colored in *red*.

† 3 Belknap, N. H. 119.

But on the other hand, the new-come planters soon felt the sore need of meadow land and pasturage, not to be found on the sandy Point itself, nor in its convenient vicinity within their own grant. Across the wide waters to the south, however, reposed unoccupied a country of virgin beauty, heavily timbered with primeval forests, and fringed all round its watered sides with emerald fields, and meadows both salt and fresh. It was very natural that the Hilton Point planters should soon fall into the easy way of ferrying their flocks and herds across the river to graze upon these vacant lands. Before long they came to mowing grass and felling timber and planting the fields; and then one after another put up dwellings and barns and entered into full adverse possession of the territory, now embraced in Newington and Greenland. Legal title to these forests and meadows, we believe, they had none. In after years, it is true, these trespassers undertook to rest their title upon some ancient Indian grant, but, as is well known, Indian deeds to New England lands were not in law held to be any better "than the scratch of a bear's claw." They occupied these lands, in the beginning, as *vacuum domicilium*, in the absence of any effective opposition from the true owners.

Let us then enquire, *who were the real proprietors* of these Rockingham County lands at the time the Hilton Point planters trespassed upon them.

As a preface to this enquiry, we need to state, that in Nov. 1629, about four months prior to the execution of the Hilton Patent, a large tract of territory, situated in the present State of New York around Lake Champlain, had been granted by the Grand Council to Sir Ferdinando Gorges, Capt. John Mason and seven other associates.* This province was named *Laconia*, by reason "of the great Lakes therein."

The design of the Laconia adventurers was to seize upon and engross to their own profit the rich peltry traffic of that vast region, then in the hands of the French and the Dutch. It was believed, in the absence of accurate knowledge of the interior country, that Lake Champlain (then called the *Iroquois*) could be reached from the New England coast by a journey of about 90 miles, and that only a narrow *portage* separated it from the head waters of Piscataqua river. Under this delusion, the Laconians hired the buildings which had been put up seven years before by David Thomson at the smaller mouth of the Piscataqua, and established there, under command of Capt. Walter Neale, a factory or entrepot, as a basis for their magnificent designs upon the New York lakes. The company of Laconia were in the actual possession of Pannaway at Little Harbor when Hilton and his company sailed up the river to establish

---

* See the Patent of Laconia, Jenness' Isles of Shoals, 2nd Ed. p. 180.

their plantation at Hilton's Point eight miles above. And before Hilton's title was perfected by *livery of seizin*, Strawberry Bank had begun to be settled; no less than sixty men were employed in the company's business on the Piscataqua,* and a plantation had been established at Newichwannock, not far from Quampegan Falls, and on the opposite side of the river from Hilton's grant. It seems to us obvious from these considerations, that the character and extent of the Hilton patent must have been familiarly known and understood by the Company of Laconia and the considerable body of men in its employment.

The Laconia adventurers expended a great deal of time and money in quest of an easy way from the Piscataqua to their coveted *El Dorado* of beaver and otter skins, but all their efforts miserably failed, and after a struggle of some two years, their design was finally abandoned.†

But during these two years' occupation of Piscataqua river, the Laconian associates had acquired

---

* Adams' Annals of Portsmouth, 18.

† We will add here, as a piece of curious information, that although the original design of the Laconians to reach Lake Champlain by ascending the Piscataqua was so soon abandoned, yet *their patent* of the province of Laconia was never, it seems, surrendered nor forfeited, but was considered as vesting in them a valid subsisting title down almost to the period of our Revolution. Jonathan Carver, who visited Lake Champlain in 1767, writes in the well-known account of his travels, as follows:

"A vast tract of land between the two last mentioned lakes (Lakes Champlain and Ontario) was granted in the year 1629 by the Ply-

an accurate knowledge of that region and its many advantages for traffic and commerce; and now, upon the failure of their original designs upon Laconia, the same body of associates, nine in number, resolved to turn their future efforts towards the development of the Piscataqua itself in the way of the fisheries and the lumber trade and of such moderate peltry traffic as could be prosecuted in the vicinity.

As the Laconia Patent conveyed to the adventurers no portion of Piscataqua river, nor indeed any territory whatever within the present State of New Hampshire, it was their first care to procure a grant of the desired region, or at least so much of it as had not been previously conveyed to Edward Hilton and his associates.

Accordingly, the same nine men, who constitu-

mouth company * * * to Sir Ferdinando Gorges and to Capt. John Mason."

"This immense space was granted by the name of the Province of Laconia to the aforesaid gentlemen on specified conditions and under certain penalties; but none of these amounted in case of emission in the fulfilment of any part of them to forfeiture, a fine only could be exacted."

"On account of the continual wars to which these parts have been subject from their situation between the settlements of the French and the Indians, this grant has been suffered to lie dormant by the real proprietors. Notwithstanding which, several towns have been settled, since the late war, on the borders of Lake Champlain and grants made to different people by the Governor of New York of part of these territories which are now become annexed to that province." (Carver's Travels p 173.)

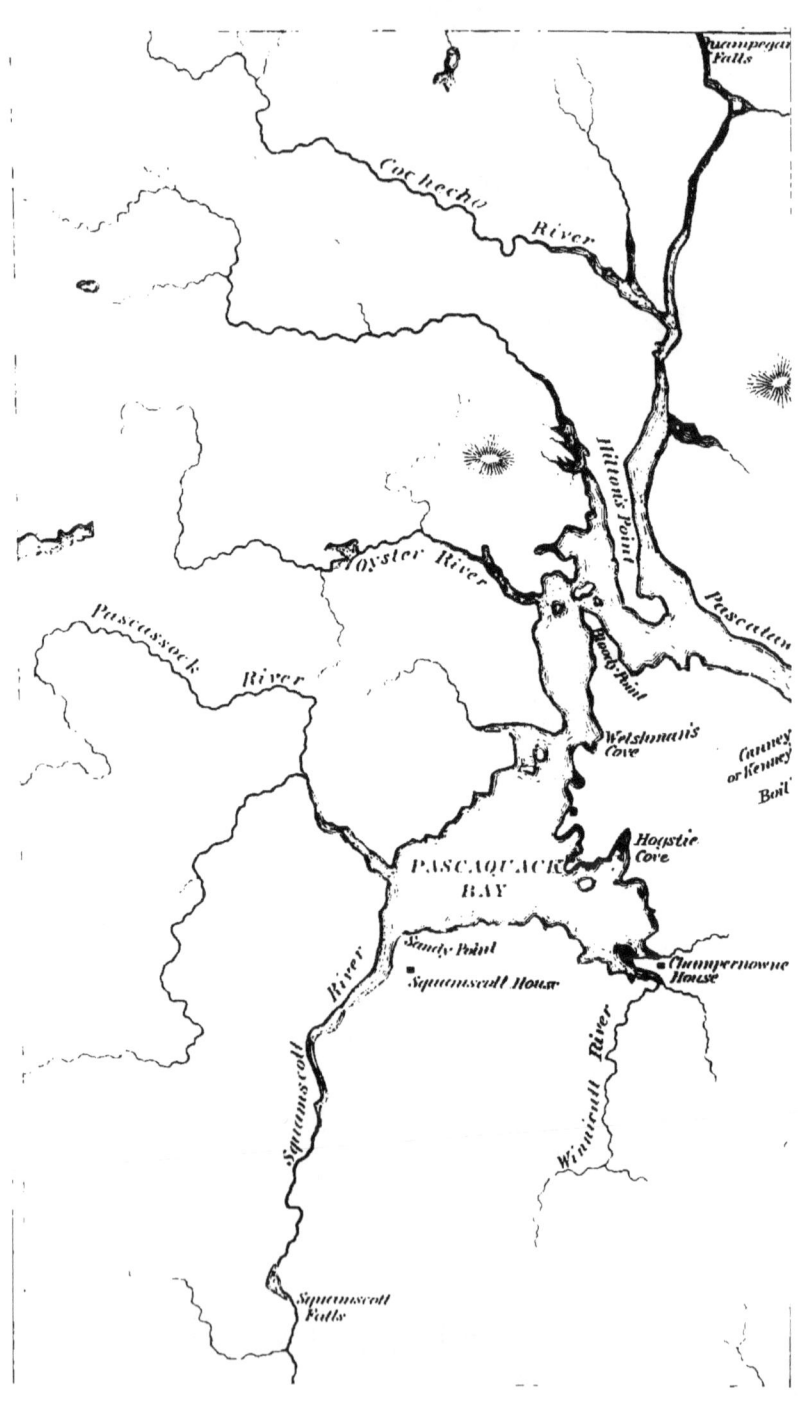

ted the Company of Laconia, procured from the Grand Council a conveyance, dated Nov. 3, 1631, (some twenty months later than the Hilton Patent,) of a considerable territory on both sides of the Piscataqua river. This important Patent, entitled "the Grant and Confirmation of Pescataway," hitherto unknown to our historians, except from a brief and grossly inaccurate abstract in Hubbard's printed history, was discovered by the writer a few years ago among the English Archives, and will be found in the Appendix.*

There is not the slightest difficulty in running out the boundaries of this "Grant of Pescataway," as will be apparent from an inspection of our Sketch map of the Piscataqua country, on which the two river patents are laid down. The river called *Pascassocke* in the description is the same, no doubt, now named *Lamprey River*, which empties into the head of Great Bay at New Market. By the terms of the Patent, the boundary line, it will be seen, ran through the middle of the Bay, called *Pascaquack* (now Great Bay) *in a westward and southwestward direction* to the bottom or lower falls of the river Pascassocke. The Lamprey is the only river, which answers to this description. Indeed, the original Indian name of the river was Piscassett;† and that name has been retained by

---

* Appendix No. 2.
† Farmer and Moore's Col. p. 50.

its principal branch, in the form of *Piscassic*, even to the present day.

The boundaries of the territory covered by the "Grant of Pescataway" began at or near Rye Ledge, not far from the present southerly line of Rye, and sweeping around the coast into the mouth of Piscataqua river, continued up the river to Fox Point, thence to Great Bay and through the middle of Great Bay to Lamprey River lower falls, and thence across the country about nine miles to the point of beginning; together with the Isles of Shoals and a strip of land three miles wide along the northerly side of the river.

So much of the Pescataway Grant as lay on the southerly side of the river and around Great Bay is now embraced in the towns of Portsmouth, Newington, Greenland, New Castle and Rye.

It will be seen, on a comparison of Hilton's Patent with the "Grant of Pescataway," that there is not the slightest conflict between them, as we have laid down the two conveyances. The Pescataway Grant expressly mentions and locates the Hilton Plantation and carefully excludes it from the conveyance. The two patents are thus entirely consistent with each other and stand well together. Both of them were executed by the same grantor, the Grand Council, some of whose most active and efficient members were then maintaining a considerable establishment on the Piscataqua, and were entirely familiar with its topography, as the minute accuracy of the description in their patent clearly attests. Neither ignorance nor mistake can be reasonably imputed to the Grand Council, nor to either set of grantees in the two river patents.

We may be morally certain that these patents did not conflict at all with each other, and that the Hilton Patent was not understood between the parties to it to cover any portion of the "Pescataway Grant." Nor do we believe that any such pretence would ever have been set up, but for the appearance upon the scene of a new Power—the government of Massachusetts Bay.

The Great Charter of Massachusetts Bay had been granted by King Charles I. March 4, 1628-9 —antedating thus both of the Piscataqua patents as well as Capt. Mason's Patent of the Province of New Hampshire which had been issued Nov. 7, 1629. In the summer of 1630, Gov. John Winthrop with a considerable company of colonists, brought the Charter over to New England. It was, indeed, a grand resounding Charter, but the extent of territory embraced within it was almost ludicrously disproportionate to this large document. Its sea-coast hardly stretched to forty miles; and more than the half of even that scanty line—to wit: from near Salem to the Merrimack—seems to have been the property of Capt. John Mason.*

---

* Jenness' Orig. Docs. p. 75. Title of Robert Mason.

Very naturally therefore, did the Founders of the
Bay Colony begin at once on their arrival to feel
about for more land and to scan attentively the language of their Charter. On the south they found
themselves hemmed in by their friends, the Plymouth colony; the west was a wilderness difficult
of access. It was thus to the north that their
hearts most earnestly yearned. The same year of
Winthrop's arrival, the Mass. colony, it is said, violently seized upon Mason's patent of Cape Anne,
"stretching their bounds three miles to the North-
wards of Merrimack River, and turned the servants
and tennants of the said John Mason out of their
possessions."*

They next cast their eyes over the Piscataqua
region, which they particularly coveted. "Because
ye river of Pascataqua is very beneficall for plantacon," writes George Burdett in 1638, "having
also an excellent harbour, wch may much pfit or
anoy them in case of warre. therefore they (the
Massachusetts) endeavour with all their skill &
might to obtain the comand thereof."†

A plausible pretext for the annexation of the desired region was found in the somewhat ambiguous
language of their Charter. By its terms they were
granted "all the lands which be within the space
of three English miles to the northward of the

---

* Jenness' Orig. Docs. p. 75.   Title of Robert Mason.
† Id. p. 31.

river, called Merrymack, or to the norward of any and every part thereof." The Massachusetts at once contended with great ingenuity, that under these terms their northern boundary reached a parallel of latitude drawn three miles above the most northerly point on the Merrimack river—a construction which would include Captain Mason's Patent of New Hampshire, and all of Maine below Clapboard island in Casco Bay.

It is here to be repeated that the Charter of Mass. Bay passed the seals March 4, 1628-9; thus antedating Mason's Patent of New Hampshire as well as *both* the Piscataqua river grants. If the Massachusetts construction of their Charter should prevail, then all of the patents on the river would be swept away; the whole of that region would fall by prior title into their hands and jurisdiction; and neither Mason, nor Hilton and his associates, nor the grantees of "Pescataway" could have offered any effectual opposition.

This ingenious interpretation of the Charter having been hit upon, there appeared as early as 1631 upon the banks of the Piscataqua, one *Capt. Thomas Wiggin*, a stern Puritan and a confidential friend of Governor John Winthrop of Mass. Bay. We find Wiggin writing from that place to Gov. Winthrop in Oct. 1631, persuading the latter to take revenge on a party of Indians for a murder committed on Walter Bagnall, called *Great Wat*, at Richman's isle. There is an implication in this request, that jurisdiction over the offence was in Mass. Bay, although Richman's island lies almost as far north as Portland harbor. The governor, however, says Winthrop, "thought best to sit still awhile."*

At this time (Oct. 1631) no special grant of the lands around Great Bay had been issued; the "grant and confirmation of Pescataway" being dated in Nov. 1631, in usual course would not reach New England until the early spring of 1632. In 1632, however, upon the arrival of the new Patent of "Pescataway," a collision occurred between Capt. Wiggin and Capt. Walter Neale, the latter acting in behalf of the Pescataway grantees. Hubbard informs us, that Wiggin, being forbidden by Neale "to come upon a certain point of land, that lieth in the midway betwixt Dover and Exeter. Captain Wiggin intended to have defended his right by the sword, but it seems both the litigants had so much wit in their anger as to wave the battle, each accounting himself to have done very manfully in what was threatened; so as in respect not of what did, but what might have fallen out, the place to this day retains the formidable name of Bloody Point."†

Hubbard does not inform us what and whose title it was, which Wiggin intended to defend, but

---
* 1 Winthrop, 63.
† Hubbard's Gen. Hist., p 217.

as at that time he had no interest whatever in the Hilton Patent, even though that Patent could be construed to cover Bloody Point, it seems clear that he could only have set up as against Neale that title, which, as we have seen, he had already asserted, and which he spent his whole after life in maintaining—the title of Mass. Bay under their great Charter of 1628.

As the construction the Bay Colony put upon their charter would, if enforced, have swept away the entire property of all the Piscataqua planters, it must have encountered a hot and determined opposition from the whole river. The Massachusetts perceived that the Piscataqua planters were bitterly hostile to them in political and religious principles, and would on that account be likely to receive efficient aid from the old country, in case of an open conflict. Again, they must have known that the real intention of the King was only to grant them as their northern boundary a strip of land three miles wide *following the course* of the Merrimack river. The strip or selvage of that breadth, was intended, we suppose, to protect the river from the artillery of any adjoining province —the range of artillery of that day being usually computed at three miles. The Privy Council, as the Massachusetts well knew, were inimical to the Bay Colony, and would seize with avidity upon the slightest transgression of their chartered limits or corporate powers, as a ground for vacating the charter itself.

In these difficulties, the Bay Magistrates deemed it prudent to break up and confuse, if possible, the solid front of opposition, before making an open attack; and to that end they resolved to get into their own hands the entire Hilton Patent. and thus extinguish the hostility of its present proprietors to their schemes and desires.

Accordingly, after concerting the plan with Gov. Winthrop and his assistants Capt. Wiggin shortly after his quarrel with Capt. Neale went out to England in 1632, and forming a company of *"honest men,"* as Winthrop calls them, succeeded, with their aid, in purchasing from Hilton and his Bristol associates the entire Hilton Patent, at the price of £2150. The purchasers were Lord Say, Lord Brook, Sir Richard Saltonstall, Sir Arthur Hazlerigg, Mr. Whiting and other men of Shrewsbury, all of them Puritans and friends to Mass. Bay, who had been "writ unto," we are informed, "by the Governor and Magistrate of Massachusetts, who encouraged them to purchase the said lands of the Bristol men, in respect they feared some ill neighborhood from them."*

Capt. Wiggin, appointed manager for the new company, returned to New England with reinforcements and supplies, and a "godly minister," arriving at Salem Oct. 10, 1633.

---
* N. H. Prov. Pap. 157.

As soon as he had entered into possession of the newly purchased territory, he took immediate steps, in accordance with the original understanding, to submit that territory to the jurisdiction of Massachusetts. Early in the following month he wrote to Gov. Winthrop "that one of his people had stabbed another and desired he might be tried in the Bay, if the party died. The Governor answered, that if Pascataquack lay within their limits (as it was supposed) they would try him."*

Before the next winter was passed, Capt. Wiggin again wrote to the Governor of Massachusetts, offering jurisdiction over crimes committed at the river, to the Bay Colony. "The Governor," says Winthrop "and divers of his assistants met and conferred about it, but did not think fit to try them here."†

The fact is, the scheme to purchase the Hilton Patent and then turn it over to Mass. Bay, had for the present utterly failed. Wiggin found it impossible to deliver his territory according to the bargain and understanding.

Intense hostility against their design sprang up at once among the original Hilton Point planters, who were in occupation of the ground. Edward Hilton was himself a royalist and a churchman, and the planters brought over by him during the

---
* 1 Winthrop, 116.
† Id. 155.

period the patent was in his hands, were naturally of the same feather. These men had now taken up and improved the lands on Bloody Point and around the easterly side of Great Bay in considerable numbers, though without any legal title to them whatever. But, as none of the patents of the Piscataqua country, not even that of Capt. Mason of the Province of New Hampshire, conferred any rights of government and jurisdiction, but were all of them simply indentures or deeds of territory, it is obvious that there were no courts or tribunals on the land, before which these *squatter rights* could be called in question; and of course the trifling value of these little properties would deter any resort to the King in Council. The squatters upon the Piscataqua thus found their possessory titles practically unquestionable, so long as they kept aloof from Massachusetts. But on the contrary, if Massachusetts were permitted to stretch her boundaries over the river, in her train would come organized courts of Law, before which land titles could be brought up for trial. This view must have been appalling to most of the planters. These squatter planters could produce in Court no instruments of title to their lands; nor had their possession been long enough continued to raise a prescriptive title. What reasonable hope of protection then could they place in a Massachusetts Court on the trial of a real action brought by the favored proprietors of the Hilton Patent? In this emergency the planters, threatened by a common calamity, gathered together for resistance to Capt. Wiggin's designs, and with such vigor did they carry on the contest, that those designs were for a time baffled; and by a sort of petty revolution Wiggin was deposed from his office as Governor, to which he had been appointed by the proprietors of the Patent, and the people set up an independent government among themselves, under the name of a *Combination*. In that year, 1637, George Burdet, a staunch churchman, succeeded Wiggin as Governor. In 1638, that inconsistent, unstable character, Capt. John Underhill, having been disfranchised, brought under admonition and banished from Massachusetts, came to Dover and was chosen Governor over the Combination, upon the understanding, no doubt, that his principles were hostile to the Bay. After Capt. Underhill had held his office about three years, however, his principles or interests in that matter underwent a change. Although a new Combination was drawn up, dated Oct. 1640, and was signed by Underhill himself, the people soon discovered that he was plotting, after all, to bring the Piscataqua under the Mass. jurisdiction,* and following the lead of Thomas Larkham, a conformist clergyman, they raised another rebellion in the interest of their independence.

---
* 1 Winthrop, 27.

The quarrel, embittered by religious dissensions, waxed hot and came to open violence. Hanserd Knollys, who was the minister of the Underhill faction, fulminated a bull of excommunication against Larkham; and in return Larkham knocked off Knowles' hat. Captain Underhill and Knowles flew to arms, expecting help from the Bay, and "so marched out to meet Mr. Larkham, one carrying a Bible on a halberd for an ensign—Mr. Knowles being armed with a pistol. When Mr. Larkham saw them thus provided, he withdrew his party and went no further, but sent down to Mr. Williams, Governor of Strawberry Bank for assistance, who came up with a company of armed men, and beset Mr. Knowles' house, where Capt. Underhill was, kept a guard upon him night and day till they could call a court, and then, Mr. Williams sitting as judge, they found Underhill and his company guilty of a riot and set great fines on them and ordered him and some others out of the Plantation."*

During the long continuance of these broils and dissensions, Massachusetts still hesitated to seize violently upon the Piscataqua. They feared the opposition of the planters under the river patents, to which we have already referred. They dreaded the bitter hostility of the numerous persons who had been banished from the Bay on account of

---

* Hubbard, 363.

their Antinomian principles, and taken refuge on
the Piscataqua; they feared, perhaps, the vengeance
of Sir Ferdinando Gorges, and his grantees, whose
territories in Maine would also be absorbed by the
Mass. construction of their charter. But the Bay
magistrates never permitted their claim over the
Piscataqua to fall into oblivion. In 1636, for instance, Gov. Winthrop wrote to Dover, that if the
latter dared to receive any persons that had been
"cast out" from the Bay, it would be taken ill, and
threatening them, that if such exiles were received,
"they should survey their utmost limits and make
use of them."*

But now at last, in 1640, amidst the turmoils and
bitter quarrels among the inhabitants, Massachusetts saw her long awaited opportunity to spread
her jurisdiction over the Piscataqua. The Company of Laconia had long since broken up; the
grantees of Pescataway had nearly all of them
withdrawn from further interest in the country;
Capt. John Mason, the patentee of New Hampshire, had died in 1635, leaving that Province to an
infant grandson; and all fear of the royal interference was dispelled amid the fast growing dissensions in the old country. Again the planters
on the upper Piscataqua were, as we have seen,
torn and paralyzed by civil and religious dissensions; and those on the lower plantation, who since

---

* 1 Winthrop, 276.

Mason's death had laid claim to the ownership of the lands on which they resided, though without any legal title, and now lived in terror of Mason's heir, even *they*, though antipodal in every sentiment to the Bay Puritans, were inclined to seek protection for their property from the strong arm of the Massachusetts.

In this propitious juncture of affairs, Massachusetts sent forward to the Piscataqua the famous Hugh Peters, with two others, "to understand the minds of the people, to reconcile some differences between them and to prepare them."* Peters spent a considerable time on the river, and upon his return in the spring of 1641, reported to Gov. Winthrop, that the Piscataqua people were, in his own words, "ripe for our Government, as will appear by the note I have sent you. They grone for Government and Gospel all over that side of the Country. Alas! poore bleeding soules."†

The precise methods used in *preparing* the people for the Puritan annexation have never been fully disclosed. Edward Hilton's assent was purchased by a covenant from the Massachusetts, that his estate should be ever after exempt from county rates.‡ Gov. Francis Williams of the lower plantation was secured for the measure, writes Peters,

---

* 2 Winthrop, 38.
† 6 Mass. Hist. Col. (4th ser.) 108.
‡ Mass. Archives, vol. 100, p. 133.

but the manner is not revealed. The chief inducement, however, held out to the population at large, seems to have been the promise of the Bay Colony, that they should "enjoy all such lawfull liberties of fishing, planting felling timber as formerly they have enjoyed in the said ryver."*

The general propositions having been settled upon, a committee was appointed on the part of the Piscataqua planters to come to an agreement with the agents of the Massachusetts upon all the various terms of the annexation. Such an agreement was soon arrived at, and thus at last the entire Piscataqua region passed in 1641, under the jurisdiction of Mass. Bay.

The formalities adopted in perfecting the transaction were, first to procure from the then proprietors an absolute conveyance to the Massachusetts Colony of the jurisdiction over the Hilton Patent. This conveyance was made June 14, 1641, and executed by George Willis, gent. and others in behalf of the rest of the patentees;† and was followed the next October by an Act of the Mass. Gen. Court, accepting and declaring "the ryver Pascataquack" to be within the jurisdiction of the Massachusetts.‡

It is now, in 1641, that we first hear of the

---

* 1 N. H. Prov. Pap. 159.
† See the Instrument, Appendix No. 3.
‡ Appendix No. 4.

strange distorted construction of the Hilton Patent, which ever afterwards seems to have prevailed.

It will be remembered that the territory, really covered by the Hilton Patent, was, if our views are correct, only that small portion of the Piscataqua, extending from Dover Point to Quampegan falls and three miles back into the country. But such a narrow construction was by no means sufficient for Massachusetts, if the submission of that patent was to be relied on as a justification for their seizure of the entire river. It became necessary to seek some widely different construction from ours, in order to stretch the patent over the lands on the opposite side of the river down to its mouth. The Massachusetts and the patentees of the Hilton Patent easily found means to make such a construction in a slight ambiguity of its terms, to explain which we must invite a moment's careful attention to the topography of the country.

The Piscataqua river, taking its rise from the Wakefield ponds, descends in a southeasterly course and passes Hilton's Point (now Dover Point) on the lower or easterly side. At this prominent neck it meets a large body of water coming down at ebb tide from the westward, and then the two flow on together to the ocean, about seven miles below. As one ascends this large western body of water from Dover Neck, he reaches, about a mile above it, a prominent Point, now called *Fox Point*—so named, according to tradition, from the circumstance that, in olden times, when the country-side was up for a fox hunt, it was the custom to beat over a considerable extent of the neighboring cover and drive the game out upon this sharp promontory, from whence, as a fox never takes the water, there was no escape. At Fox Point, the river turns sharp about, at an acute angle, and ascending in a southerly direction expands into a lake, now called *Great Bay*, about four miles wide at its upper end. Great Bay is a tidal lake, not at all dependent upon the Piscataqua for its waters. At high tide, when this large basin is filled by the sea, the prospect over its pellucid surface, framed all around with green meadows and waving grain and noble woods, is truly enchanting. But when the tide is out, a vast bed of black ooze is exposed to view, traversed here and there by narrow canals, bearing the scanty waters of the several small streams, which empty into this great lagune. One of the largest of these streams, coming from the south and emptying into the upper extremity of this lagune, is now called Exeter river, and some five miles above its mouth are the *Squamscott Falls*.

Now the Hilton Patent, if we recall its terms, conveyed the Point itself, "with the south side of said river [Piscataqua] up to the falls of the river and three miles into the mainland by all the breadth aforesaid."

Why might not the words, "the south side of said river," reasoned the Bay authorities, appropriately designate the line drawn from the mouth of the river up to Fox Point and thence around Little and Great Bays to Squamscott river, and thence up that river (now called Exeter river) to the falls?* Great Bay and Exeter river might be made to pass as the Piscataqua; and Squamscott falls would answer well enough for the falls referred to in the description. At all events there was no power on the river, as we have before stated, to dispute whatever construction the Massachusetts chose to put upon the instrument Accordingly, the construction we have mentioned was adopted and enacted into a law by Mass. Gen. Court, in June 1641, and made a part of the very instrument of submission, by which the Hilton Patent was put under their jurisdiction.

The language of the preamble to that convention,† was as follows: "Whereas some Lords, Knights, gentlemen, and others, did purchase of Mr. Edward Hilton and some merchants of Bristol, two patents, one called Wecohannet or Hilton's point, commonly called or known by the name of Dover or Northam, the other pattent, set forth by the name of the south part of the ryver of Pascataquack; beginning at the sea-side or near thereabouts

---

* See the Sketch Map.
† See Appendix, No. 3.

& coming round the said land by the river unto the falls of Squamscott as more fully appears by the said grant, &c." Then follows a concession to the Mass. government, of jurisdiction over all the said territory, "Provided always," continues the instrument, "& it is hereby declared that one of the said patents, that is to say, that on the south side of the ryver of Pascataquack & in the other pattent one third part of the land with all improved land in the said pattent to the Lords and gentlemen & other owners shall be & remain unto them, their heirs and assigns forever as their proper right and as having true interest therein, saving the interest of jurisdiction to the Massachusetts." "And this honored Court of the Massachusetts hearby promise to be helpful to the maintenance of the right of the Patentees in both the said Pattents in all the legal courses in any part of their jurisdiction."*

---

* Appendix, No. 3.

The preamble, it will be noted, recites that the Lords, &c., had purchased of Edward Hilton two patents, the one called Hilton's Point or Dover patent; the *other* "set forth by the name of the south part of the ryver Pascataquack, &c." Some of our ablest antiquarians have charged the Massachusetts with having designed by this phraseology to raise a false belief in the public mind, that the *Hilton Point* or *Dover Patent* was a separate and distinct instrument from that which conveyed the south side of the river, on which latter, about this time they conferred the name of the *Bloody Point Patent* or more frequently, the *Squamscott Patent*. We think injustice has been done in this matter, from not attending with sufficient care to the meaning of the word *Patent*, as used in those days. That word was employed to designate the *territory granted* as well as the *instrument of convey-*

THE PISCATAQUA PATENTS.

Now, we enquire, does the Hilton grant purport to begin "at the sea-side or near thereabout," as the Gen. Court has enacted in 1641? Does it specify the "Falls of Quamscott" as the upper limit of the grant? Does it describe the boundary as "coming round the said land by the river," as the Mass. authorities have declared? We find no such language nor any such meaning in the Hilton Patent.

Indeed, it may well be doubted whether at the the time the Hilton Patent was granted, the name *Piscataqua* was ever applied by the English or the

---

ance. Thus *Dover Patent* meant that portion of the lands conveyed by the Hilton Patent lying on the Dover side of the river; so. *Bloody Point* or *Squamscott Patent* designated the territory, construed to be covered by the Hilton Patent, which lay on the Squamscott side of the river. Indeed the land embraced within the present town of Stratham was called Squamscott Patent, until the incorporation of the town in 1715. (9 N. H. Prov. Pap. 778.) It was natural and convenient, when a Grand Council grant covered two distinct parcels of territory, that these parcels should take distinct names. The "Grant and Confirmation of Pescataway," for instance, embracing as it did lands on both sides of the river, for convenience was split into two distinct portions in common parlance, and that portion which lay on the southerly side of the river went by the name of the *Great House Patent* or *twenty thousand acre Patent*. There is no design in the preamble, above quoted, to convey a false impression that the titles to the Dover and the Squamscott Patents were founded upon two separate and distinct instruments of conveyance; but, on the contrary, the preamble expressly recites that both these tracts were bought from Edward Hilton, who, as was well known, was proprietor, with his associates, of only *one* Patent, though about this time it took distinct names for the two divisions for convenience of designation.

Indians to the Exeter River, on which the Squamscott falls are situated.* The Patent of New Hampshire, for instance, issued to Mason in 1629, applies the name Piscataqua to the main stream, which comes down over Quampegan falls. So also the "Grant of Pescataway" in 1631 uses that term in the same sense.

---

* The Indian name of our noble river was, as nearly as it can be expressed by English letters, *Paskataquauke*—or otherwise *Paskataquagh*—the last syllable being pronounced with a guttural sound and a forcible expulsion of the breath, not capable of representation by our letters, but closely resembling the sounds of the Gaelic or some of the Oriental tongues. This syllable *quauke* or *quagh* is clearly the Indian word *auke* signifying *a place* or *locality*—a word found scattered abundantly all over the Abenaki country, in combination with various descriptive prefixes. The prefix *Pa-skata*, as the Indians seem to divide the word, (with a strong accent upon the last syllable,) we have recently been led to believe signifies a *branch, division, separation*.

Some fifteen years ago, as we are informed by Rev. Dr. Alonzo H. Quint of Dover, there happened to be a small party encamped at Dover Point, one of whom was then an Indian undergraduate in college, or recently graduated. Elder Samuel Sherburn, of Barrington, was there at the same time, engaged in the melancholy search for the body of his son, who had been lost off a *gundalow* at Boiling Rock. One day Elder S, asked the educated Indian the meaning of the name "Piscataqua." The Indian at once held up three extended fingers and said, "you see that? well, three rivers make one," referring of course to the fact that the two main branches of the Piscataqua and the Bellamy or Back river, all meet together at Dover Point.

A few days after receiving this information from Dr. Quint, the writer chanced to meet on the steamboat that plies between the Shoals and Portsmouth, two Oldtown Indians on their return to the Penobscot. They were both men of middle age, apparently intelligent, and could converse, though with some difficulty, in English. On my enquiry of them as to the signification of "Piscataqua"

Looking again carefully at the Mass. legislative construction of the Hilton Patent, we are curious to know what has become of the twenty-five square miles or thereabouts, really granted by that instrument, as we understand it. We find its entire rear boundaries carried away; nothing is left of the territory except what might pass under the two

(which they pronounced Pa-skata-quauke,) their answer was prompt and unpremeditated. Holding up their hands and extending two or three fingers, just as had been done by the Indian at Dover Point, they said *Pa-skata* meant a *branch* or division of the river into two or more parts—the whole word Paskataquanke meaning a place where boats and canoes *ascending* the river together from its mouth were compelled to separate according to their several destinations. Since that interview, the writer has conversed, on the same subject, with another party of Indians encamped for the summer at the Farragut House, Rye Beach. Their translation of the word *Piscataqua* was the same as above given. And that definition is also confirmed by Thoreau, who informs us in his "Maine Woods" on the authority of an Abnaki Indian, that *Piscataquis*, the name of a river in that State which empties into the Penobscot above Bangor, signifies "*branch of a river*," in the Abnaki dialect.

It will be remembered that some of the permanent settlements of the Indians were at the falls of Squamscott, Piscassocke (Lamprey) and Shanhassick, (Oyster river,) the way to which lay up the *western* branch of the Piscataqua waters, and other settlements lay at *Newicek-wan-auke* (*my wigwam place*), access to which was up the *eastern* or main branch of the river. The water course to the Indian habitations at Cochecho falls and along Bellamy or Back river, lay on the north and the north-west sides of the same Hilton's Point. That Point was thus to the Indians the most important and most striking natural object on the river. From the convenience of access to this conspicuous promontory for all the river Indians, it must always, we think, have been the chosen scene for the gathering of all the tribes, for their powwows and their war-dances, and their green corn-dances and their general assemblies for purposes of war or the chase.

words "Hilton's Point"—at the utmost a few acres of barren ground, quite inadequate to the purposes of a trading and lumbering plantation such as Hilton intended to establish.*

Another serious consequence of this construction, if carried out, would have been the confiscation of almost the entire peninsula on the south side of the river, granted in 1631 to the nine

---

And it was also the place where the Indians of the various villages on returning to their homes *branched off* from each other and paddled their canoes up the pellucid streams to their several wigwams.

Whether the native tribes had any general name for the whole river does not as yet appear. Probably not, if we are to reason by analogy from their usual custom in similar cases. The word *Pascataquauke* designated the branching of the river at Dover Point, and if we may be permitted to go a little way further into these dubious speculations, we infer from the Indian names above Dover Point that the branch of the great river particularly designated by that title was the westerly branch which reaches up to Fox Point and thence through Great Bay to Lamprey river. Our inference is drawn from the Indian names of these latter bodies of water. Great Bay was called by them *Pascaquack*, and Lamprey river bore the name of *Pascassocke*, both of which words are but slight modifications of *Pascataquauke*. The easterly or main branch of the river from Hilton Point to the Cochecho was called by them the *Winnakahannet*; above the Cochecho to the Great Falls it was named *Newichwannock*.

It was, we suppose, by the English that the word Piscataqua, applied by the aborigines only to the branching of the stream at Dover Point, was first used to designate the entire river from its source in the Wakefield ponds to its mouth.

* The Point must be carefully distinguished from the Neck. The former name as appears from Dover Records, we are informed by Dr. Quint, was always confined between the very end of the promontory and a low huckleberry swamp, a short distance in the rear.

Laconia adventurers. The plantation at Little Harbor, all the buildings, lands and improvements at Great Island and Strawberry Bank, the result of large expenditures of money and ten years of labor and hardship, would have passed into the hands of the proprietors of the Hilton Patent, without the slightest compensation.

The Mass. construction of that Patent was, however, never fully carried out, as we shall see in the sequel. The chief purpose of that construction was to furnish the Bay Colony with such a pretext of jurisdiction over the New Hampshire plantations, as, in combination with the ambiguous terms of their own charter, might justify or excuse the advance of their northern limits to the banks of the Piscataqua. A few preliminaries having then been arranged, such as conferences with the inhabitants and the procurement of signatures to petitions for union with the Massachusetts, the latter colony, in Oct. 1641, took all the south Piscataqua plantations into their government, and retained them for nearly forty years, until, in 1679, New Hampshire was reclaimed from the Massachusetts by the King, and erected into a Royal Province.

On finally draughting the Statute of annexation, the question arose for determination, whether the Piscataqua should be taken into the Bay jurisdiction upon the *voluntary submission* of the planters and patentees of the Hilton Patent;

or whether jurisdiction over that region should be assumed, as being *within the Massachusetts bounds.** Feeling, we conjecture, that their title to the river under the Hilton patent, just submitted to their jurisdiction, was at least questionable, if not clearly worthless, the sagacious government of the Bay resolved, now that opposition was disarmed, to rest their right to the Piscataqua upon the vigor of their own charter. This position was highly advantageous for the Massachusetts, as it was already meditated to advance their chartered limits across the Piscataqua far north into the Province of Maine, upon the strength of that same construction of their charter. Accordingly, the Act of Annexation, consummated Oct. 9, 1641, making no mention whatever of the Hilton Patent, nor of the surrender of jurisdiction over it by its proprietors, nor of the voluntary submission of the people, though by these means only had the Massachusetts got the control of the river, now, in the preamble, rests the Massachusetts title upon the sole and simple declaration, that the annexed territory lay within the original chartered limits of the Bay Colony;† and it is thereupon enacted "that from thenceforth the said people inhabiting there (on the river Pascataquack) are and shall be accepted and reputed under the Government of the

---

* 2 Winthrop, 42.

† Appendix, No. 4.

Massachusetts as the rest of the inhabitants within the said jurisdiction are."*

Now that the jurisdiction of the Bay Colony had, in the way we have described, been securely extended over the long coveted Piscataqua, the Massachusetts had little or no further interest in the river patents, and no doubt would gladly have withdrawn from any further intermeddling in the matter. But difficulties and injustices of many sorts soon sprang up all over the annexed territory, which long disturbed the quiet of the new Gov-

---

* By the terms of this statute of annexation of Oct, 1641, certain privileges were guaranteed to the Piscataqua people, as an inducement, no doubt, to their yielding to Mass. jurisdiction. One of these was that "the inhabitants there are allowed to send two deputies from the whole ryver to the Court at Boston." This article was one of prime importance to the Piscataqua people, and flattered them with the hope that under its provisions they were really to secure a representation in the Gen. Court at Boston. This hope proved quite delusive as to the planters of the lower Piscataqua. The Act of Union undoubtedly granted them a right to send a deputy to General Court, but the laws of Massachusetts, it was found, rejected all deputies except freemen of their colony and members of the Congregational church in good standing. Now, as there was not for some years after the annexation any congregational church gathered "in a church way" at Strawberry Bank or Great Island, there were no suitable deputies to be found on the lower river. (1 N. H. Prov. Pap. 167.) Those benighted people succeeded in finding among them "a godly man" from Massachusetts, named James Parker, and him they deputed to Gen. Court in 1642 and 1643. In 1644, they sent Mr. Stephen Winthrop; but with the exception of these three years, no deputy came from the lower Piscataqua until the year 1653 (Id. 367); by which time the control of that region had fallen entirely and absolutely into the hands of the Puritan friends of Massachusetts.

ernment. Only a slight outline of these feuds and contentions, however, will the general subject of this paper permit us to present here.

The inhabitants of Bloody Point in particular, who had formerly crossed the river from Dover, as before stated, now found themselves in danger of being stripped of their farms. Under the Mass. contract with the owners of the Hilton or Squamscott patent, the latter's title to the whole of these lands was acknowledged and warranted by Act of Gen. Court, and more than this, upon the laying out of the limits of Dover in 1642, it would seem that the whole of Bloody Point was excluded out of Dover township, so that these now isolated planters had neither title to their farms, nor the protection of any organized town government, nor any rights in the town common lands. In these straits they applied earnestly to the General Court for relief, and the latter, whose favor to the proprietors of the Squamscott Patent was fast fading away, granted their prayer, and in 1643, an Act was passed, that "all the marsh and meadow grounds lying against the great bay or Strawberry Bank side shall belong to the town of Dover, together with 400 acres of upland ground adjoining or lying nere to the said meadow."* This Act was passed without the consent and against the protests of the proprietors of the Hilton Patent.†

* 1 N. H. Prov. Pap. p. 172.
† Id. 158.

The following year (1644) the Mass. Gen. Court granted to the township of Dover the entire neck of land, known as Bloody Point, bounded on the southward by a line drawn from Canney's creek to Hogstie Cove.* (See Sketch Map.) This latter grant, like the former, was made, it would seem, in disregard of the rights of the owners of the Hilton Patent, towards whom, now that the jurisdiction of Massachusetts had become firmly fixed over the Piscataqua, the friendship of the latter had sensibly cooled.

So, too, the inhabitants of Strawberry Bank, though by the Act of 1641 all their estates were liable to seizure by the proprietors of the Hilton, or then more generally called Squamscott Patent, manfully struggled against that Patent and defied Capt. Wiggins "to bring his Pattent to this present Court."† And some of the Dover people, even after the considerable concessions above mentioned had been made them, maintained a hostile spirit to the Hilton Patent, as it had been construed, declaring in their Petition of 1654, that this "Patent wee conceive, (under favor) will be made voyde if it be well looked into."‡

Meantime, in the twenty years and upwards since the Puritan Lords and gentry of Shrewsbury had

---

* 1 N. H. Prov. Pap. 175.
† Id. 207.
‡ Id 213.

purchased the Hilton Patent for the convenience of Mass. Bay, its ownership had in various ways passed mostly into the hands of other proprietors, some of whom were by no means friendly to that colony. The property had been originally divided into twenty-five shares of one hundred pounds each, which shares passed from hand to hand by bills of sale, many of which are still to be found on record. At the period to which we have now arrived, from 1650 to 1656, the Hilton Patent had thus come to be largely owned in various proportions by a considerable number of New England persons, among whom were the Quaker, Nicholas Shapleigh, Edward Colcord, a man subsequently convicted by the Massachusetts "of many notable misdemeanors and crimes,"* and others perhaps of similar stripe.

On the other hand, the lower plantation on the Piscataqua had, since 1641, undergone a complete transformation, civil and religious. A party of strict Puritans had, by the aid of the Massachusetts, gotten possession of that plantation, and under the system of the Bay Colony were enabled to perpetuate their power at their own pleasure, and to allot among themselves—some eight or ten in number—nearly all the valuable common lands within their limits. If we may trust the language of a petition to the King made in 1665, by some of the non-freemen of Portsmouth, "five or six of

---

* 1 N. H. Prov. Pap. 238.

the ritchest men of this parish ruled, swaied and ordered all offices both civil & military at their pleasure." These men, continues the petition, "have kept us under hard servitude, and denyed us in our publique meeting the Common prayer Sacramts and decent burial of the dead," "and not only so, but have also denied us the benefit of freemen * * and likewise at the election of officers, the aforesaid party * * have always kept themselves in offices for the manageing of the gifts of lands & setling them * * and have engrossed the greatest part of the lands within the precincts and limits of this plantation into their own hands, and other honest men, that have been here a considerable time have no lands at all given to them."*

In this posture of affairs, it was not to be expected that the shareholders of the Hilton Patent should receive any further special favor from Massachusetts, as against the Piscataqua settlements. For a considerable time, indeed, the General Court declined, though urgently petitioned, even to order a partition of the Patent, but at last, in 1655, the Court partially yielded and appointed a Committee "to make a just division of the (patent) of Squamscott only & that which hath reference to Dover be respited untill another time."†

The Report of this Committee,‡ made the fol-

* Jenness' Orig. Docs. rel. to N. Hamp. p. 48.
† 1 N. H. Prov. Pap. 217.
‡ Id. 221.

lowing year, in view, no doubt, of the impolicy if not impossibility of making a partition of all the territory declared to be within the Patent by the Act of 1641, proceeds upon the idea of effecting a compromise among the now numerous and discordant interests.

In the preamble, the Committee first lay down the extent of territory to be divided. They do not pretend to quote the exact language of the Patent, but content themselves with putting their own construction upon it. "When we came to peruse the Pattent," they say, "we found it to extend for the length of it from the lower part of the river Pascataquack on the south side of said river unto the falls of said river at Exeter and for breadth along the said river 3 miles from the falls of the head-line for the breadth of it."

The last clause of this description is, as it stands, utterly unintelligible. The obscurity seems to have been caused by the negligence of the transcriber of the Report. It so happened that in our researches among the original Mass. Records, we came upon *another* report of the Partition Committee made about a week before the Report finally adopted. As this first Report, not having been acted upon, was not printed among the Mass. Records, it has escaped the notice of our antiquaries. The preamble to the first Report,* which was obvi-

---

* The most striking difference between these two Reports consists

ously intended to be copied into the second, supplies the words (here printed in italics) which are necessary to give that second Report a meaning. Its language is this: "when we came to peruse the patent, we found itt to extend for the length of itt from the lower part of the river Pascataquack on the south side of the said river unto the falls of said river at Exeter; and for breadth along the said river *three miles into the land, upon which wee measured* three miles from the falls for the Head Lyne for the breadth of itt."*

On comparing the preamble to this final Report (as corrected) with that of the Act of Submission of 1641, we find a material variance between them. By the former, the Hilton patent only reached down to the *lower part* of the river, while by the Act of Submission it is declared to begin "*at the sea-side or thereabouts.*" In their Report, the Committee fix upon *Boiling rock* as the lower boundary of the patent on the river, and in this easy and arbitrary manner, the entire settlements below Boiling Rock were excluded from the patent.

---

in this, that by the first nothing whatever is allowed out of the Patent to the Dover people or to the planters upon Bloody Point, though considerable tracts had been granted them in 1643 and 1644 by Act of Gen Court. We suppose it was this strange or crafty omission which roused the people of Dover and Bloody Point (then a part of Dover) to active resistance to the adoption of the Committee's first Report; and led to the amended Report, which was finally approved.

* 3 Mass. Archives, 452.

The committee, in their final Report, also except out of the patent all the extensive lands granted to and incorporated with Dover by the Mass. Gen. Court, together with a hundred and fifty acres added; and they also restrain the limits of the patent along the easterly part of Great Bay to a depth of one and a half miles into the land, instead of the three miles allowed by the Act of 1641; on the ground, they say, that "the land was so narrow to the seaward, that we can allow no more according to the intent of the Patent as we understand it." It seems plain that the Committee in making their partition, acted and assumed to act not as judicial officers, but rather in a spirit of compromise, in the hope of composing the long standing dissensions among the Piscataqua planters.

Their scheme was to satisfy as far as possible, or at least to appease all the conflicting interests in the Squamscott territory. To the lower plantation they granted all the land below Boiling Rock; to Dover they confirmed the territory on Bloody Point and around Great Bay, which had been granted to the town in previous years; to the proprietors of the Hilton or Squamscott Patent they reserved only the remainder, which they then proceeded to divide up among the three classes or ranks of these proprietors in the general manner, as we understand the Report, designated upon the accompanying Sketch Map. The portion colored upon the map in *yellow* was assigned to the "Shrewsbury men;" that in *blue* was laid off to Capt. Thomas Wiggin and his partners;* that in *red*, which had long since been granted by Massachusetts to Dover, was confirmed to that township, and that colored *green* was allotted to Gardiner, Lake, and their partners.†

The partition thus made of the Hilton or Squam-

---

* It is curious to notice, on comparing the northern boundary of Capt. Wiggin's portion with the southerly bound of the "Pescataway Grant," how nearly, if not precisely, they correspond. The Great Bay would, of course, constitute the natural northern bound of the second division granted to Wiggin and his partners, and it is difficult to understand why the committee adopted the limit laid down in their Report, unless they were acquainted with the bounds of the Pescataway Grant, and desired to keep the Captain's own lands out of harm's way against any contingencies.

† The various localities marked upon our sketch map, indispensable to any clear understanding of our subject, have been ascertained from documents, records, statutes, &c. with as much of care and pains as the difficulty of the research required.

Canney's Creek or *Cove* (erroneously called Kinges Creek in the printed Report of partition) lay on the Long Reach of the Piscataqua, about half a mile above Boiling rock, and next below the lower bound of the ancient Rawlins farm, still in possession of that family. Its exact location appears from the terms of the grant made by Portsmouth in 1661, to Capt. Brian Pendleton of a tract of 240 acres of land "next to James Rawlins," "which takes its beginning," says the record, "at Kenney's cove and runs down by the riverside 80 rods to Pyne cove and thence into the woods 480 rods to the edge of the Pitch pine plain upon a W. S. W. Lyne." (1 Ports. Rec. p. 77.) The several grants made about the same time to other persons, of all the remaining lands down the river to Boiling Rock, establish the distance of Canney's cove above that prominent land mark. The reason why this little cove was selected as the lower boundary of Bloody Point was, we conjecture, that it just embraced the land of James

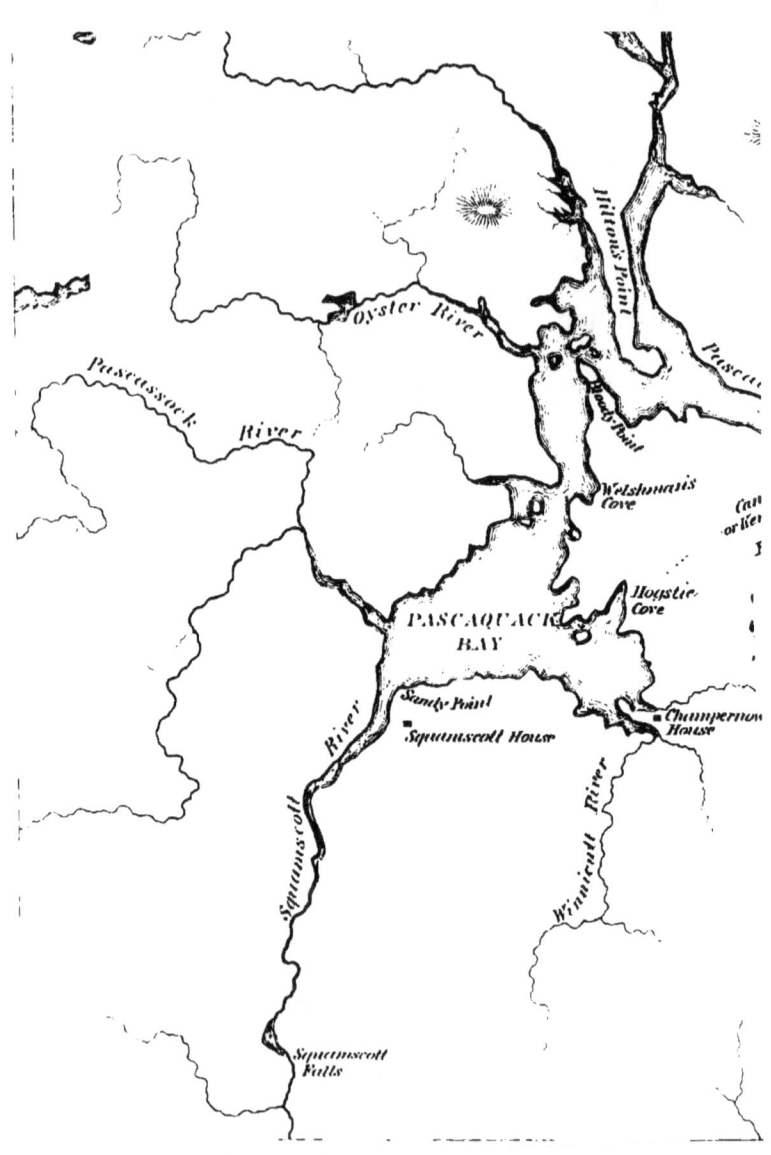

scott Patent in 1656, as we have described it, was accepted as final so far as it related to the two portions set off to the "Shrewsbury men" and to Captain Wiggin—those colored on the map in *blue* and in *yellow*. As to these portions there had never existed any conflicting title, except that of Rawlings, an early and influential Dover man, whose farm had the cove for its lower boundary.

"*Hogstye Cove*" is ascertained from the terms of a survey made by Portsmouth in 1695. Mr. George Snell and William Vaughan, the surveyors, "run the line," they report, "from Canney's Cove in the longe rech to Hoggstye cove at the mouth of ye great Bay, and from the middle of the mouth of ye one cove to the middle of ye mouth of ye other is West and by South and East & by North and strikes Mr. William Furber's Barne." (1 Ports. Rec. p. 330.)

Welshman's Cove on the Little Bay is still known as *Welsh Cove* among the ancient families in the vicinity.

The entire neck of land lying above the line drawn from Canney's Creek to Hogstye Cove was originally called, from the circumstances of the quarrel between Captain Wiggin and Neale, before referred to, *Bloody Point*—a name still retained by a projection into the river nearly opposite Dover Point.

"*Cotterill's Delight*" was a location at the extreme south-east corner of Great Bay near the mouth of Winnicot river, or perhaps Packer's creek. (1 N. H. Prov. Pap. 208, 222. 1 Ports. Rec. Anno 1666.) We have been unable to discover the origin or meaning of this name.

The site of *Captain Champernowne's house* upon the magnificent farm of the late Col. Joshua W. Peirce at Greenland, is still pointed out to the delighted antiquary. Here dwelt for many years, in something of antique breadth and state, that relative and almost companion of Rawleigh and Gilbert; that noblest born and bred of all New Hampshire's first planters.

Grand old English oaks, planted, as tradition has it, by the Captain's own hands, still lift their brave vigorous heads over the fertile meadows—true Herne's oaks, we exclaimed at the first glance—

John Mason and his heirs under his patent of New Hampshire—a title, which, in the then political condition of England under Cromwell, hardly amounted to a cloud.

The remainder of the Hilton or Squamscott patent, as laid down by the Committee, lay wholly within the Pescataway Grant.* But though the

---

unique in New Hampshire—a scene as beautiful as that from Windsor castle over Datchet Mead.

The ancient name, *Sandy Point*, is retained to the present day. Not far from this Point is still discernible the cellar of the famous *Squamscott house*. Capt. Thomas Wiggin, so often referred to in these pages, as the constant friend of Mass. Bay, erected this house about 1650, and here he died in 1667. For fourteen years he had held the high office of Assistant to the Governor of Mass. Bay; the only Piscataqua man, we believe, ever chosen to that position. Having, in 1651, purchased of Thomas Lake a large interest in the Squamscott Patent, there was alloted to him and his partners, (who subsequently released their interests to him,) a territory three miles square, along Exeter river, now embraced in the town of Stratham In close proximity to the "Squamscott House," in a field which slopes north towards the Bay, and almost upon the northern boundary of his land, are buried the bodies of that grim, sturdy Puritan and several generations of his family. The present owner of this burial ground, a lineal descendant of Capt. Thomas, conducted us to the cemetery. Headstones, footstones, inscriptions, were all gone. Great maples and oaks were growing over the ancient *God's acre*; dead leaves rustled along the weird and shadowy ground. As the Puritan had in his life resembled Joshua, the son of Nun, who lead the children of Israel into a land flowing with milk and honey, so, like Joshua was he fitly buried "in the border of his inheritance, in Timmath-serah, on the north side of the hill of Gaash."

* This latter grant was still held as the cherished property of the town of Portsmouth. Even so late, for instance, as 1660, Portsmouth appointed Commissioners to run out the line between that town and Hampton, "always provided," says the record, "that not

owners of the Pescataway or Great House Patent had, as we have argued, a superior title to the whole peninsula, embraced within their limits, yet in the present posture of affairs, now that all the land below Boiling Rock was reserved to them by the Committee for Partition, it was deemed better by John and Richard Cutt, Capt. Brian Pendleton, Richard Martyn, Joshua Moodey and the few others who then ruled the lower plantation under the Massachusetts, to negociate peaceably for the purchase of the small remainder of land, left to the Squamscott proprietors, than to undertake a probably fruitless appeal to the Courts of Law. Having resolved on this course, the above named gentlemen so managed the affair, that in a few years they themselves became owners of nearly the entire tract.

In 1658, or before that year, the selectmen of Portsmouth bought of Thomas Lake the entire tract of land between Kenney's creek and Boiling Rock, on the river, and running back nearly a mile and a half into the land "to the edge of the pitch pine plain upon a W. S. W. Lyne." The consid-

---

any of the lands belonging to the Great House Patent be granted to be in the township of Hampton by those empowered by us." (1 Ports. Rec. p. 66.) The Great House Patent seems to have been the familiar title of the old "grant and confirmation of Pescataway," so far as it applied to the southerly side of the river. This southerly section of the Pescataway Grant appears also to have been sometimes entitled the "Twenty Thousand acre patent." (1 N. H. Prov. Pap. 83-96.)

eration *paid by the town* was £50. In 1661 this large tract was divided and laid out among Capt. Brian Pendleton and his associates;* 240 acres each to Capt. Pendleton and John Cutt, 80 acres to Joshua Moodey, and 52 acres to Richard Martyn.

The large and valuable tract stretching from Winnicut River along Great Bay to Sandy Point seems to have lain unappropriated until 1669, at which time the town, having determined to assert their own superior title over it against the Squamscott patentees, granted two-thirds of the entire tract to John Cutt, Nathaniel Freyer, Capt. James Pendleton and others, "provided," continues the Record, "the parties abovesaid maintain and defend the same in the towne's behalf at their, the aforesaid parties owne proper cost and charge against any that shall oppose—further that the town grants and confirms unto Mr. Andrew Wiggin the right and title to his land, as was granted to him by Capt. Lake and Capt. Waldron with the priviledges of our town, provided wee recover the land aforesd by law."† A few grants to private individuals seem also to have been made by Lake and Waldron out of their portion of the Squamscott Patent, but on quite nominal considerations.

In these several ways, the pretended claim of the Hilton Point proprietors to any of the land

---

* 1 Ports. Rec. p. 51-68-77.
† Id. p. 135.

covered by the " Grant of Pescataway," or " Great House Patent," was at last extinguished, or repudiated, and nearly the whole of that territory (except what remained to Dover) fell into the hands of a knot of men at Portsmouth, as rapacious as they were harsh and bigoted.

As to the " *Dover Patent,*" or northerly portion of the Hilton Patent, as it was construed by Massachusetts, we do not find that any steps were ever taken to lay out and bound the land covered by it, but the township of Dover having been partly bounded out in 1642, shortly after the union of the Piscataqua to Massachusetts, received in 1656, concurrently with the partition of Squamscott, a quit claim from the planters of all their interest in Dover, with a slight reservation of about 16 acres.*

The only substantial advantage derived from the Mass. construction of the Hilton Patent was taken by the Massachusetts themselves. Jurisdiction over the Piscataqua had been obtained by the skilful use of that instrument, and when once got, it was firmly kept, after that instrument had disappeared. But this usurpation, of which it has been said "a more unjust and tyrannical act never was perpetrated on this continent,"† was not destined to endure for many years. The people of the lower Piscataqua were in spirit deadly hostile to the

---
* 1 N. H. Prov. Pap. 223.
† Potter's Hist. of Manchester, p. 116.

Mass. Bay. Shortly after the annexation, a few of the Puritan sort and faith had crept into the country, and by the aid of the Bay had seized on the offices and places of power and appropriated to themselves nearly all the common lands; but the original planters grew daily more and more incensed. In 1651, the inhabitants of Strawberry Bank openly rebelled and attempted to withdraw their subjection to the Boston government.* But this outbreak was suppressed. Another effort was made to the same purpose on the arrival of the Royal Commissioners in 1664, though without permanent success. But in 1679, the Massachusetts usurpation over the Piscataqua was terminated by the erection of New Hampshire into a Royal Province.

Thus did the last fruits of the Hilton Patent decay and perish; thus were the angry broils of forty years composed. The proprietors of the Patent had after all profited little or nothing by the attempted appropriation of Piscataqua lands; the Massachusetts were in the end compelled to disgorge the purloined jurisdiction they had so uneasily obtained and kept, and thus retributive justice was at last meted out to all the actors in the transaction.

In conclusion and recapitulation of the views presented in this monograph, we have endeavored

---
* 1 N. H. Prov. Pap. 195.

to show, that it was the desire of Mass. Bay to include the Piscataqua region within her limits and to secure there a good neighborhood of "honest men," which led her magistrates to effect, through their friend Capt. Thomas Wiggin, in 1633, a purchase and transfer of the Hilton Point Patent to the Puritan Lords and gentlemen of Shrewsbury; whose successors in 1641, in accordance, we suppose, with the original understanding, made a full submission of the Patent to Mass. jurisdiction. At the same time, in furtherance of the same general design, a statutory construction was put upon the Patent, by which it was split into two distinct portions, and the lower or Squampscott portion was violently stretched so as to cover the whole southern bank of the river from Squamscott falls to its mouth.

The Hilton Patent having thus served its political and religious purpose, was never fully enforced. Large portions of its territory were granted to Dover and a still larger part was retained by Strawberry Bank, and in the conclusion of the whole matter, the Squamscott patentees took but trifling advantage from the distorted misconstruction of their grant.

The long controversy was no doubt of trifling importance, but whoever will study it attentively will see displayed such a stubborn conflict between patentee and planter; such a hot contention between Royalist and Roundhead; such fierce hatred between Puritan and Churchman; and at all times such political sagacity and vigor of thought, as make the story of the Hilton Point Patent (only a brief outline of which we have sketched) the most instructive if not entertaining in the early annals of New Hampshire.

The real history of New Hampshire during the first half century of its existence has not yet been written. Until a very recent date, the only original materials for such a history, available to our students, were the scanty relics of our town and county records, and a few documents preserved among the Archives of Massachusetts or in private hands together with some casual hints and prejudiced notices of the Piscataqua to be found among the historians of Plymouth and the Bay. Dr. Belknap's narrative of this early period, founded upon materials such as these—the only ones, however, at his command—could at best have drawn a mere outline of its history; and now it turns out that even the outline of our early history made by that elegant historian is utterly mistaken and distorted. The annals of New Hampshire from the time of its first planting down to its erection into a royal province, in 1679, require to be entirely rewritten. A great mass of new materials for that purpose has lately been gathered together by our antiquarians, and now await only the kindling pen of an impartial historian to shed a clear and satisfactory light over the tortuous ways and the dark mysteries of our early history.

APPENDIX.

I.

The Hilton or Squamscott Patent.

To all X'rian People to whome these presents shall come, Greeting, [after the usual recital of the great grant by King James in 1620,] Now know yee that the said President and Councell by Virtue & Authority of his Majties said Letters Pattents, and for and in consideracon that Edward Hilton & his Associates hath already at his and their owne proper costs and charges transported sundry servants to plant in New England aforesaid at a place there called by the natives Wecanacohunt otherwise Hilton's point lying some two leagues from the mouth of the River Paskataquack in New England aforesaid where they have already Built some houses, and planted Corne, And for that he doth further intend by Gods Divine Assistance, to transport thither more people and cattle, to the good increase and advancemt & for the better settling and strengthing of their plantacon as also that they may be the better encouraged to proceed in soe pious a work which may Especially tend to the propagacon of Religion and to the Great increase of Trade to his Majties Realmes and Dominions, and the advancement of publique plantacon. Have given granted Enfeoffed and Confirmed, and by this their p'sent writing doe fully clearly and absolutely give grant enfeoffe and Confirme unto the said Edward Hilton his heires and assignes for ever, all that part of the River Pascataquack called or known by the name of Wecanacohunt or Hilton's Point with the south side of the said River, up to the fall of

the River, and three miles into the Maine Land by all the breadth
aforesaid. Together with all the Shoares Creeks Bays Harbors and
Coasts; alongst the sea within the limitts and Bounds aforesaid with
the woods and Islands next adjoyneing to the said Lands, not being
already granted by the said Councell unto any other person or persons together alsoe with all the Lands Rivers Mines mineralls of what
kinde or nature soever, woods Quarries, Marshes, Waters, Lakes
flishings, Huntings, Hawkings, flowlings, Comodities Emolumts and
hereditaments whatsoever withall and singular their and every ol
their Appts in or within the limitts or bounds aforesaid, or to the
said Lands lying within the same limitts or Bounds belonging or in
any wise appertaining. To have and to hold, all and singular the
said Lands and p'mises, with all and singular the woods Quarries
Marshes, Waters, Rivers, Lakes. flishings, flowlings, Hawkings.
Huntings, Mynes, Mineralls of what kynde or nature soever, priviledges, Rights Jurisdicons Libbertyes Royalties and all other proflits
Comodities Emoluments and hereditaments whatsoever, before in
and by these p'sents given and granted, or herein meant intenconed
or intended to be hereby given or granted, with their and every of
their appts and every part and parcell there of (Except before Except-
ed) unto the said Edward Hilton his heires, Associates and Assignes
forever to the onely proper use and behoofe of the said Edward Hilton his heires Associates & Assignes for ever, yielding and paying
unto our Soveraigne Lord the King one flifth part of Gold and Silver
Oares, and another flifth part to the Councell aforesaid and their successors to be holden of the said Councell and their successors by the
rent hereafter in these p'sents Reserved, yielding and paying there-
for yearly for ever unto the said Councell their successors or Assignes
for every hundred Acres of the said Land in use the sume of twelve
pence of Lawfull money of England into the hands of the Rent gath-
erer for the time being of the said Councell yr successors or Assignes
for all services whatsoever, And the said Councell for the affaires of
New England in America aforesaid, Doe by these p'sents nominate
Depute, Authorize appoint and in their place and stead put William
Blackston of New England in America aforesaid clerk William Jef-
fries and Thomas Lewis of the same place Gent and either or any of
them Joyntly or severally to be their true and Lawfull Attorny or
Attorneys and in their name and stead to enter into the said part or
porcon of Land, and other the p'mises with the appts by these p'sents

Given and granted or into some part thereof in the name of the whole, and peaceable & quiett possession and seisin thereof for them to take and the same soe had and taken in their name and stead to deliver possession & seisn thereof unto the said Edward Hilton his heires Associates and Assignes, according to the tenor forme and effect of these p'sents Ratifieing Confirmeing and allowing all and whatsoever the said Atorny or Attornyes, or either of them shall doe in or about the p'mises by virtue hereof. In witnesse whereof the said Counceli for the affaires of New England in America aforesaid, have hereunto caused their common Seale to be putt the twelfth day of March Anno Dmi 1629. And in the fifth yeare of the Reigne of our Soveraigne Lord Charles by the Grace of God of England Scotland, ffrance and Ireland, defender of the ffaith &c.

RO: WARWICKE.

Memo: that upon the 7" day of July Anno Dmi 1631 Annoq: R's Caroli pri: Septimo: by virtue of a warrt of Attorny within menconed from the Councell of the affaires in New England under their Comon seale unto Thomas Lewis he the said Thomas Lewis had taken quiett possession of the within menconed p'mises and Livery and Seisen thereof hath given to the within named Edward Hilton in the p'sence of us.

Vera Copia Efficit pr nos   Thomas Wiggin
Tim: s Nicholas   Wm. Hilton
Pet Coppeer   Saml Sharpe
     James Downe

Vera Copia
    Attest   Rich: Partridge, Cler.
[Endorsed]

Grant from the Councell of Plymouth to Edward Hilton of Lands in New Hampshire in New England dated the 12" March 1629.
For Hilton's Point And the south side of said River & to the falls.
Allen vs. Waldron
Feb'y 1704—5.

II.

Grant and Confirmation of Pescataway to Sr. Ferdinando Gorges and Capt. Mason and others, Ano 1631.

THIS INDENTURE made the 3d day of Novemr Ano Dni 1631: and in ye 7th year of ye Reigne of Our Sovraigne Charles by the Grace of God of England Scotland France and Ireland King Defender of the ffaith &c. Betweene the Presidt & Councill of New England on ye one pty and Sr Ferdinando Gorges Knt Capt John Mason of London Esqr and their Associates John Cotton Henry Gardner, Geo: Griffith Ehwin Guy Thomas Wannesseth Thomas Eyre and Eliezer Eyre on ye other pty Witnesseth [after reciting the Great Patent of King James to the President & Council of New England, dated Nov. 3, 1620,] that the sd Presidt and Councill of their full free and mutuall consent, as well to ye end that all the Lands Woods Lakes Loucks, Rivers, Waters, ponds Islands and Fishings, wth all other Traffique Proffits and Commodities whatsoever to them or any of them belonging, and hereafter in these Pnts mencioned may be wholly and entirely invested appropriated secured and settled in and upon ye sd Sr ffardinando Gorges, Capt John Mason and their Associates John Cotton, Henry Gardner, George Griffith, Edwyn Guy, Thomas Wannerton Thom Eyrie, & Eliezer Eyre as by diuers speciall Services by them already done for the aduancement of the sd Plantacon by makeing of Clap board and pipestaues makeing of Salt Panns and Salt, transporting of Vines for makeing of Wines searching for Iron Oare being all businesse of uery great Consequence for causeing of many Soules both men, women and boys and store of Shipps to be employed thither, and so in short time proue a great Nursery for Shipping and Mariners, and also a great helpe to such as in this Kingdome want good Imploymt And further for Yt the sd Sr fferd Gorges Capt. John Mason and their said Associates John Cotton Henry Gardner Geo. Griffith Edwin Guy Thom: Wannerton Tho Eyre and Eliezer Eyer have by their Agents there taken great paines and spent much tyme in the discouery of the Countrie all wch hath cost them (as we are credibly Informed) 3000lb and upwards, which hitherto they are wholly out of purse upon hope of doing good in time to come to ye publique, And also for other good and sufficient Causes and Consideracon the sd Presidt and Councill especially thereunto moueing, HAUE given granted bargained sold assigned aliend, sett ouer enfeoffed and confirmed and by these pnts Do giue grant, bargaine sell assigne, aliene sett ouer enfeoffe and confirm unto the sd fferdinando Georges Capt John Mason John Cotton Henr Gardner Geo Griffith Edwin Guy Thom. Wannerton Thom. Eyere and Eliezer Eyre, their Heirs and Assignes for euer All that house and chiefe habitaco͞n situate and being at Pascataway als Pascataquack als Pascaquacke in New England aforesaid, wherein Capt Walt. Neale and ye Colony wth him now doth or lately did reside togeather wth the Gardens and Corne ground occupied and planted by the sd Colonie, and the Salt workes allready begun as aforesd. And also all that porco͞n of Land lying wthn the precincts hereafter menconed, beginning upon the Sea coast 5 miles to the Wtward of or from the sd chiefe Habitacon or Plantation now possessed by the sd Capt Walter Neale for ye use of the Adventurers to Liconia (being in the latitude of 43 Degr or thereabouts in the Harbour of Pascataquack als Pascataquack als Passataway, and so forth from ye sd beginning Eastwd & North Eastwd and so proceeding Northwds or North Westwds into ye Harbour and Riuer along the Coasts and Shoares thereof including all the Islands and Isletes lying wthn or neere unto the same upwards unto the head land opposite unto the plantacon or Habitacon now or late in the Tenure or Occupation of Edw Hilton & from thence wt wds & South wt wds in ye midle of the Riuer and through the midle of ye Bay or Lake of Pasquacack als Pascaquack or by what other name or names it hath toward the bottome or Westermost part of ye Riuer called Pascassocke to the falls thereof, and from thence by an Imaginary Line to pass ouer, and to the Sea, where the Prambulacon begann Togeather wth all ye Lands, Soyle, Ground Wood, Quarries, Mines fishing Hunting Hawking fowling Comodities and Hereditamts whatsoeuer, Togeather also wth all prrogatiues, Jurisdicco͞ns Royallties, priuileidges, ffranchises and preheminence wth in ye precincts of Land conteined wthin ye limits or bounds aforesaid. And also the Isles of Shoales, and ye ffishings thereabouts And all the Seas wthin 15 miles of that̄ oresd Sea Coast. And also all the Sea Coast and Land lying on ye East and North east side of the Harboure and Riuer of Pascataway aforesd and opposite to the bounds aboue mencioned begining 15 miles to ye S. eastward of ye Mouth or first entrance and begining of the said Harboure,

and so upp to ye falls and into the ponds, or Lakes that feed the sd
ffalls, by the space of 30 miles including the sd ponds or Lakes
and the Shoores thereof, and so crossing into the Landward, at a
right angle by the space of 3 miles the whole length thereof from ye
sd mouth or first entrance from the Sea and Eastwds into ye Sea wch
sd 3 miles shalbe allowed for ye breadth of ye sd land last menconed
both upon ye land and sea, As also all ye land Soyle Ground Woods,
Quarrie, Mines, flishings Hunting Hawking flowling Commodities
and Hereditamts whatsoener, togeather wth all prerogatines Juris-
diccons Royallties, Prinileidges, ffranchises and prheminence wthin
the preincts of Land last menconed, conteined To haue and to hold
all ye sd House and Habitacon porcons of Land and all Lakes and
Islands therein conteined as aforesaid, and all and singular other ye
prmisses hereby given, granted, bargained, sold, aliened, enfeoffed,
and confirmed, wth all and singular the appurtences and euery part
and peell thereof unto ye sd Sr fferdenando Gorges, Capt John Mason, John Cotton, Henry Gardner Geo. Griffith, Edwyn Guy, Thomas Wannerton, Thomas Eyre and Elyezer Eyer to ye only use & behoofe of them ye sd fferd. Gorges &c their Heires and Ass. for
euer. Yielding and paying unto our Souer Ld ye King his Heires
and Successors 1-5 of all ye Oare of Gold and Siluer that from time
to time and at all tymes hereafter shalbe there gotten, had & ob-
teined for all seruices, duties and Comands, and also yeilding & paying unto the sd Presidt Councill and their Successers euery yeere
yeerely for euer 40s sterl. at ye ffeast of St Mich: tharchangell if it
shalbe lawfully demanded, at the Assurance House on the West side
of the Royll Exchange in London. [Then follow the usual cove-
nants for quiet possession and further assurance—and the appoint-
ment of Capt. Thom. Camock and Henry Joselin as attorneys to
deliver seizin and possession.] In Witnesse whereof the said president and Councill to two parts of these presents both of One Tenor
haue sett their Common Seale and to one part thereof the sd Sr
Ferden: Gorges, Capt. John Mason, John Cotton, Henry Gardiner,
Geo: Griffith, Edwyn Guy, Tho: Wannerton Thom: Eyre and Eliezer Eyre haue sett their hands and Seale the Day and yeere first
aboue written.

(Endorsed in pencil) 3. Nov. 1631.

N. Engd.

APPENDIX. 85

[Note.]

Previous to our discovery of this instrument, our knowledge of its terms was derived solely from the abstract printed in Hubbard's Gen. Hist. of New England, p. 215. Hubbard had evidently seen a true copy of the instrument which he states was then extant (*circa* 1680) in the hands of some gentlemen living at Portsmouth. He quotes accurately considerable portions of the document; but when he undertakes to set forth a condensed description of the limits of the Grant, his language, *as printed*, is misleading or unintelligible. The text is as follows: "Among other things there is also added [to the Pescataway grant] salt works, lying and being situate near the harbor of Pascataqua with all the lands adjoining, that run along five miles westward by the sea-coast, and so to cross over in an angle of three miles breadth towards a plantation in the hands of Edward Hilton supposed to be about Dover and so towards Exeter."

This description is absolutely *without meaning*. What signification can be attached to the words, "*and so to cross over in an angle of three miles breadth towards a plantation in the hands of Edward Hilton?*" And, moreover, this description, as it stands printed, purporting to be copied out of the Patent itself, is on its face erroneous, for how could a Grant, made in 1631, refer to the town of *Exeter*, which was unknown and unnamed until several years later?

We may be confident that the Rev. William Hubbard did not write any such description of the "Pescataway Grant," as is printed in his history, and that the jargon of his printed language has been introduced by the ignorance or carelessness of his transcribers, or by the impossibility of deciphering at times "Hubbard's crabbed autograph." As is well known, the "General History of New England" was printed by the Mass. Hist. Society from a manuscript which once belonged to Prince. This manuscript was not in the author's own handwriting, and different portions of it were copied by several different transcribers, some of whose chirography is illegible to the most careful study. Under such circumstances, the printed History could hardly escape numerous errors which, though they have severely shaken the authority of the work, are not justly chargeable against the "learned and ingenious author" himself.

Whoever will take the pains to compare Hubbard's description of the "Grant of Pescataway," above quoted, with the language of the Instrument itself, will be satisfied that he had before him a copy of that instrument at the time he extracted his description from it, because the words used in this description are nearly all of them to be found in the Grant. The description, as printed, purports from its inverted commas to be quoted literally from the instrument itself. This is obviously incorrect, as Hubbard undertakes only to give the *substance*, not the language, of the grant.

What were the exact words used by the historian in making up his epitome of the Pescataway grant, we shall perhaps never know; but it may be entertaining, in the absence of any sort of knowledge on the subject, to indulge in fanciful conjectures. Suppose we supply to Hubbard's description the few words, here printed in *italics*, to be found in the Patent itself, but omitted perhaps by the transcriber; the clause will then read thus:

"Among other things there is also added salt works lying and being situate near the harbor of Pascataqua with all the lands adjoining, that run along five miles westward by the sea coast and *al*-so *the lands on the east side of the river*, to cross over *into the landward* at a *right* angle *by the space* of three miles breadth towards a Plantation in the hands of Ed. Hilton supposed to be about Dover and so towards Exeter."

The description, as thus amended, would be an intelligible and generally accurate abstract of the limits of the Pescataway Grant.

III.

Paper of Submission.

The 14th of the 4th mo. 1641.

Whereas some Lords, knights, gentlemen & others did purchased of Mr. Edward Hilton, & of some merchants of Bristoll two pattents, one called Wecohannet or Hilton's point commonly called or knowne by the name of Dover or Northam, the other pattent set forth by the name of the south part of the ryver of Pascataquack beginning at the sea side or near thereabout & coming round the said land by the river unto the falls of Quamscott as more fully appear by the said grant: And whereas also the inhabitants residing at present within the limitts of both the said grants have of late & formerly complained of the want of some good government amongst them & desired some help in this particular from the jurisdiction of the Mass Bay, whereby they may be ruled and ordered according unto God both in church & commonweal, and for the avoyding such insufferable disorders whereby God hath been much dishonored amongst them. Those gentlemen whose names are here specified, George Willis gent, Robt. Saltonstall gent, Will. Whiting, Edward Holliock, Thomas Makepeace, partners in the said pattent do in behalfe of the rest of the patentees dispose of the lands & jurisdiction of the premises as followeth, being willing to further such a good worke have hereby for themselves & in the name of the rest of the pattentees given up & set over all that power of jurisdiction or government of the said people dwelling and abiding within the limitts of both the said pattents unto the government of the Massachusetts Bay, by them to be ruled & ordered in all causes criminall and civill as inhabitants dwelling within the limitts of the Massachusetts government & to be subject to pay in church & commonweale as the said inhabitants of the Massachusetts bay do & no other. And the freemen of the said 2 pattents to enjoy the like liberties as other freemen do in the said Massachusetts government, & that there shall be a court of justice kept within one of the 2 patents, which shall have the same power that the courts of Salem & Ipswich have, Provided always, & it is hereby declared that one of the said pattents, that is to say that on the south side of the ryver of Pascataquack, & in the other pattent one third part of the land with all improved land in the said pattent to the lords & gentlemen & other owners shall be & remain unto them, their heirs & assigns forever as their proper right & as having true interest therein saving the interest of jurisdiction to the Massachusetts, and the said pattent of Wecohannett shall be divided as formerly is exprest by indifferent men equally chosen on both sides, whereby the plantation may bee furthered & all occasions of differences avoyded.

And this honored court of the Massachusetts hearby promise to bee heelpful to the maintenance of the right of the Pattentees in both the said Pattents in all the legall courses in any part of their jurisdiction.

Subscribed by the fore named gentlemen in the presence of the general court assembled the day afore written. C. Rec., vol. 1, pp. 304 and 5.

IV.

The Act of Union.

A General Court held at Boston the 9th day of the 8th month 1641.

Whereas it appeareth that by the extent of the line (according to our patent) that the ryver of Pascataquack is within the jurisdiction of the Massachusetts & conference being had (at severall times) with the said people & and some deputed by the Generall Court for the setteling and establishing of order in the administration of justice there. It is now ordered by the Generall Court holden at Boston the 9th day of the 8th month 1641, & with the consent of the inhabitants of the said ryver as followeth:

Imprimis, That from henceforth the said people inhabiting there are and shall be accepted & reputed under the government of the Massachusetts as the rest of the inhabitants within the said jurisdiction are.

Also that they shall have the same order and way of administration of justice and way of keeping courts as is established at Ipswich & Salem.

Also that they shall be exempted from all publique charges other than those that shall arise for, or from among themselves or from any occasion or course that may be taken to procure their own particular good or benefit.

Also they shall enjoy all such lawfull liberties of fishing, planting felling timber as formerly they have enjoyed in the said ryver.

Mr Simon Bradstreete, Mr Israell Stoughton, Mr Samuel Symonds, Mr Willi. Tynge, Mr Francis Williams & Mr Edward Hilton or any four of them, whereof Mr Bradstreete or Mr Stoughton to bee one these shall have the same power that the Quarter Courts at Salem and Ipswich have.

Also the inhabitants there are allowed to send two deputyes from the whole ryver to the Court at Boston.

Also Mr. Bradstreete, Mr Stoughton and the rest of the commissioners shall have power at the Court at Pascataquack to appoint two or three to joyne with Mr Williams & Mr Hilton to govern the people as the magistrates do here till the next Generall Court, or till the Court take further order.

It is further ordered that until our commissioners shall arrive at

Pascataquack, those men who already have authority by the late combination to govern the people there shall continue in the same authority & power to bee determined at the coming of the said commissioners & not before. C. Rec., vol. 1, pp. 319, 20.

V.

Report of Committee on Partition.

May 22, 1656.

We whose names are hereto subscribed according to an order of the honored Generall Court in November 1655, appointinge us to make a first devision of the Pattent of Swamscott doe thus make our returne.

When we come to peruse the Pattent we found it to extend for the length of it from the lower part of the river Pascataquack on the south side of said River unto the falls of said River at Exeter, & for breadth along the said River 3 miles from the falls of the head lyne for the breadth of it, which head lyne we run upon a southeast poynt of the compass which ended three quarters of a mile beyond Aspe brooke towards Hampton about 40 pole beyond or below the high way where we marked a great red oak on fowre sides.

2dly. From the said head lyne we measured for the length on the Northeast poynt of the Compass 6 miles & a halfe the which extended to that part of the bay near Winicott River.

3dly. We measured a second cross line for breadth beginning at Squamscott house extending it 3 miles upon the south east poynt where we did mark severall pine trees. The rest of the land belonging to the Pattent about & below the great bay we understood to be impassable as to measuringe by reason of the exceedinge thick swamps; but we took the best information we might of divers & severall inhabitants of the great Bay & Straberry Banke & their reports agreed viz., that from the lower part of the bottom of the Bay neere Capt. Champoun's house to the River neere the Boyling Rock or thereabout all the neck of land within that Lyne unto the little Bay Contayninge as neere as men of best experience can informe about 4 miles square being all within the Pattent. And whereas from the easterly part of the great Bay, being a part of the river, we should have measured 3 miles into the land we find in that place by credible information the land so narrow to the seaward that we can allow no more according to the intent of the Pattent as we understand it that one mile and a halfe to be run from each poynt of the bottom of the Bay upon an easterly line into ye land.

To the matter of service appoynted unto us by the Generall Courte concerning division of the Pattent, we finding the present owners to be of three sorts or ranks we have therefore agreed to make three severall divisions. The first division being 8 shares & one quarter belonging to Mr Nathaniel Gardner, Mr Tho. Lake & partners, we assign and lay out to them all the land from Bloody Point unto the boyling Rock for breadth or thereabouts & for length extendinge to the lower lyne of the middle devission which is about 40 pole from Sandy Poynt & so the lyne running Southeast 3 miles in the land as also the land lying upon the bottom of the great Bay, being or extendinge one mile & halfe from every part of the bottom of the bay upon an east'ly lyne into the woods in which division of the land & marsh graunted unto Dover by the generall Court shall be & remayne to them forever viz., the land from Kinges Creeke to a certain Cove neere the mouth of the great Bay called Hogstye Cove with all the marsh from that place round about the bay up to Cotterills Delight with 400 acres ot upland as it graunted by the Court bounded layd out and possessed by the inhabitants of Dover with 50 acres of upland more about or neere the great Bay with 50 acres to be layd out and disposed of by Capt. Richard Walden to some of the inhabitants of Dover, whom he sees fitt.

The second division being 8 shares & one quarter belonging to Capt. Thomas Wiggan & partners, who have purchased and obtained the same, we assigne & lay out 3 miles square beginning at a plump of trees standing on a peece of old planting land about 40 poles below Sandy poynt, & up the river upon a streight line toward Exeter, the River being the bounds of it on the North side & at each end to run a lyne upon the southeast poynt of the Compass 3 miles into the land there to bound it on that side, Provided that Capt Tho Wiggan pay unto the other two thirds the sum of £66 13s 4d according to their shares and proportions in boards within 6 months if demanded which he is to pay at either of his saw-mills in Pascataquack river.

To the third division being 8 shares & one quarter belonging to the Shrewsbury men, to which we assigne & lay out all that land from the uppermost lyne of the middle division to the mouth of the Creeke called Mr Wheelwrights creeke, the same to run 3 miles towards Hampton upon a southeast lyne all the land between this lyne & Exeter falls to the full extent of the Lyne to ly[e] to Exeter, being graunted to them by deed of gift by Capt. Wiggan sole agent for the Company.

The Court allows & approves of the returne of this Committee as is here exprest. } SAMUEL WINSLOW, WM BARTHOLOMEW, SAMUEL HALL.

www.ingramcontent.com/pod-product-compliance
Lightning Source LLC
Chambersburg PA
CBHW031120160426
43192CB00008B/1051